ISBN 1-74123-017-9

CONTRIBUTE TO STRATEGIC DIRECTION

by

Adelaide Institute of TAFE

Department of Management Studies

Software Publications

CONTRIBUTE TO STRATEGIC DIRECTION

Author: JACQUELINE JEPSON

Editor: MELANIE BHAGAT

ISBN: 1-74123-017-9

Disclaimer

Publishers – Software Publications Pty Ltd (ABN 75 078 026 150)

Head Office – Sydney
Unit 10, 171 Gibbes Street
Chatswood NSW 2067
Australia

Web Address
www.softwarepublications.com

Branches

Adelaide, Brisbane, Melbourne, Perth and Auckland

Table of Contents

Unit 4 Uncertainty

Unit 5 Forecasting: Qualitative Methods

Unit 6 Forecasting: Quantitative Methods

UNIT 7 Five Forces

Unit 8 Resource-Based Model

Unit 9 SWOT Analysis

UNIT 10 Glossary

UNIT 1

SYSTEM THEORY/ CONTINGENCY THEORY

Development of management theory

Management theory has evolved over time. New theories have developed as the understanding of work and people has developed and grown. Early terrorists tended to bring their existing experience and expertise into the 'new' field of management theory.

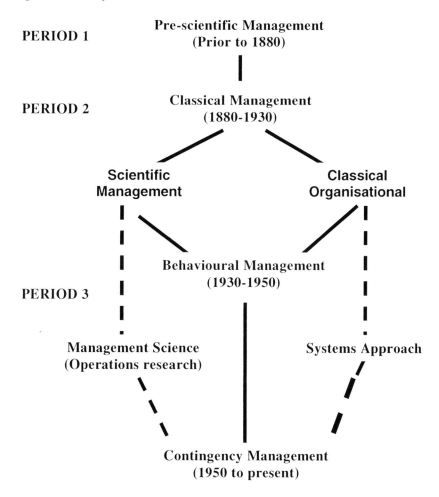

Theories are useful in that they help us to understand, explain and predict the structure and behaviour of organisations. They are not an end in themselves, but rather a tool to be used to increase a manager's effectiveness. Most theories build on other theories as ideas develop and grow.

> '*all knowledge is provisional, conjectural, hypothetical - we can never finally prove our scientific theories, we can merely (provisionally) confirm or (conclusively) refute them; hence at any given time we have to choose between the potentially infinite number of theories which will explain the set of phenomena under investigation. Faced with this choice, we can only eliminate those theories which are demonstrably false, and rationally choose between the remaining, unfalsified theories.*'

> *Source: Discussion of Karl Popper's views on "Growth of human knowledge" http://plato.stanford.edu/entries/popper/#Grow*

Organisational structures and the style of management required to make them function are a product of their social and historical context. The development of management theory can be identified as falling into four periods.

A. Pre-scientific Management

Pre-scientific management era refers to the period immediately preceding the Scientific Management started by FW Taylor and his associates. Prominent among the pioneers who made significant contributions to management thought were the following.

1. Robert Owen (1771-1858)

Owen believed workers' performance was influenced by the total environment in which they worked. Throughout his life Owen worked for the building up of a cooperation between the workers and the management. He believed and practised the idea that the worker should be treated as human beings. Owen suggested that investment in human beings is more profitable than investment in machinery and other physical resources. He introduced new ideas of human relations, eg shorter working hours, housing facilities, education of children, provision of canteen, rest pauses, training of workers in hygiene etc.

Owen is known as the father of personal management. His ideas and philosophy may be considered as a prelude to the development of behaviour approach to management

2. Charles Babbage (1792-1891)

Babbage was a professor of mathematics at Cambridge University from 1828 to 1839. Babbage perceived that the methods of science and mathematics could be applied to operations of factories. He made several contributions expounding his ideas and theories.

Babbage was a pioneer of operations research and industrial engineering techniques. He laid considerable emphasis on specialisation, work measurement, optimum utilisation of machines, cost reduction and wage incentives. His emphasis on the application of science and mathematics laid the foundation for the formulation of a science of management.

3.   Henry Vamun Poor

Poor advocated a "managerial system" with a clear organisation structure in which people could be held completely accountable and the need for a set of operating reports summarising costs, revenues and rates. He recognised the danger that such a system might make people feel like cogs in a machine. To overcome this, he suggested a kind of leadership, beginning at the top of an enterprise that would overcome routine and dullness by instilling in the organisation a feeling of unity, an appropriation of the work, and an esprit de corps. Thus Poor called for a system before Taylor. He called for the recognition of human factor before Mayo. He also suggested leadership to overcome the rigidities of the formal organisation much before Chris Argyris.

4.   Henry Robinson Towne (1844-1924)

HR Towne was president of the famous 'Yale and Towne', a lock manufacturing company. He took particular interest in studying efficient management of the business. He applied his ideas successfully in his own company. In 1886, he presented a paper the "Engineer as an Economist", wherein he urged the association of engineers and economists as industrial managers. The combination of the knowledge along with at least some skill as an accountant is essential for the successful management of industry. He suggested organised exchange of experience among managers and an organised effort to pool accumulated knowledge in the art of workshop management.

5.   James Watt (1796-1848) and Mathew Robinson Boulton (1770-1842)

Watt and Boulton were the sons of the distinguished inventor of the steam engine. They applied a number of management techniques in their Engineering Factory at Soho (Birmingham, UK). These techniques were:

- market research & forecasting
- standardisation of components and parts
- production planning
- planned machine for better workflow
- elaborate statistical records
- maintenance of advance control reports and cost accounting procedures
- provision of employee welfare with sickness benefit scheme administered by an elected committee of employees, and
- scheme for developing executives

6. Captain Henry Metcalfe (1847-1917)

Metcalfe published a famous book "The Cost of Manufacture and Administration of Workshop: Public and Private" in 1882. Metcalfe suggested "new systems control" covering the following:

(a) The science of management is based on principles that are evolved by recording observations and experiences.

(a) The art of management should be based on several recorded and accumulated observations, which are presented systematically.

(a) That management should make certain cost estimates on the basis of these observations.

(a) However management should maintain only relevant and crucial information. A manager should prepare the details of work which will then be communicated to foreman and workers.

Metcalfe suggested a system of cards. Under this system managers prepare two type of cards: time cards and material cards. This system is intended to assure the workers that good work done by them would be known to management. It also provides a method for gauging their work. The American Management Association has put Metcalfe's system of management on record.

Systems of management have been practised in one form or other ever since men started forming groups and living in civilised society. The Sumerian civilisation dating back to 300 BC had an efficient system of tax collection. The pyramids of Egypt, the Chinese Civil Service, the Roman Catholic Church and military organisations also offer good examples of early application of management. However a systematic study and analysis of management as a science began only in the twentieth century after the industrial revolution.

By far the most influential person of the time and someone who has had an impact on management service practice as well as on management thought up to the present day, was FW Taylor. Taylor formalised the principles of scientific management, and the fact-finding approach put forward and largely adopted was a replacement for what had been the old rule of thumb.

He also developed a theory of organisations, which served as the forerunner for many subsequent writers on management science.

Sources: http://in.geocities.com/kstability/learning/management/evolution.html

The industrial revolution became the catalyst for the development of management theory.

B. Scientific Management - Frederick Winslow Taylor - Theory of Scientific Management

FW Taylor is considered the "Father of scientific management" and his contributions mark a new era in Modern Management Thought. The concepts propounded by him have an impact on management service practice as well as on management thought up to the present day. Taylor formalised the *principles of scientific management*, and the fact-finding approach put forward and largely adopted was a replacement for what had been the old rule of thumb.

He also developed a theory of organisations, which has been largely accepted by subsequent Management Philosophers.

FW Taylor's Contributions to Scientific Management

By 1881 Taylor had published a paper that turned the cutting of metal into a science. Later he turned his attention to shovelling coal. By experimenting with different designs of shovel for use with different material (from 'rice' coal to ore) he was able to design shovels that would permit the worker to shovel for the whole day.

In so doing, he reduced the number of people shovelling at the Bethlehem Steel Works from 500 to 140. This work, and his studies on the handling of pig iron, greatly contributed to the analysis of work design and gave rise to method study.

To follow, in 1895, were papers on incentive schemes, a piece rate system on production management in shop management and, later, in 1909, he published the book for which he is best known, *Principles of Scientific Management*.

A feature of Taylor's work was stop-watch timing as the basis of observations. However, unlike the early activities of Perronet and others, he started to break the timings down into elements and it was he who coined the term 'time study'.

Taylor's uncompromising attitude in developing and installing his ideas caused him much criticism. Scientific method, he advocated, could be applied to all problems and applied just as much to managers as workers. In his own words he explained:

> "The old fashioned dictator does not exist under Scientific Management. The man at the head of the business under Scientific Management is governed by rules and laws which have been developed through hundreds of experiments just as much as the workman is, and the standards developed are equitable."

Objectives of Scientific Management

The four objectives of management under scientific management were as follows:

- The development of a science for each element of a man's work to replace the old rule-of-thumb methods.

- The scientific selection, training and development of workers instead of allowing them to choose their own tasks and train themselves as best they could.

- The development of a spirit of hearty cooperation between workers and management to ensure that work would be carried out in accordance with scientifically devised procedures

- The division of work between workers and the management in almost equal shares, each group taking over the work for which it is best fitted instead of the former condition in which responsibility largely rested with the workers. Self-evident in this philosophy are organisations arranged in a hierarchy, systems of abstract rules and impersonal relationships between staff.

FW Taylor's Contribution to Organisational Theory

This required an organisational theory similar for all practical purposes to that advocated by those organisational theorists who followed. These theorists developed principles of management which included much of Taylor's philosophy.

His framework for organisation was:

- clear delineation of authority
- responsibility
- separation of planning from operations
- incentive schemes for workers
- management by exception
- task specialisation

Criticism Of Theories Expounded by Taylor

Taylor's philosophy, though it gained immense popularity, was also widely criticised on three grounds.

1. Scientific management ignored the human side of organisations. Taylor viewed an average worker as a machine that could be motivated to work hard through economic incentives. Workers and Trade Unions opposed his views strongly on the plea that it was exploitative.

2. Taylor's theory is narrow in scope having direct application to factory jobs at the shop floor level. Taylor and his disciples were called "Efficiency Experts" because they concentrated attention on improving efficiency of workers and machines. Scientific management is therefore restricted in scope as a theory of Industrial Engineering or Industrial Management, rather than a general theory of management.

3. Taylor advocated excessive use of specialisation and separation of planning from doing. Excessive division of labour had disastrous consequences in the form of repetitive and monotonous jobs and discontent among workers.

Nevertheless, Taylor's theory and principles have exercised considerable influence on modern management thought. His emphasis on use of scientific methods in solving work-related problems is widely accepted by modern experts on management. Taylor's impact has been so great because he developed a concept of work-measurement, production control and other functions, that completely changed the nature of industry. Before scientific management, such departments as work-study, personnel, maintenance and quality control did not exist. What was more his methods proved to be very successful. Quantitative approach or management science approach is based largely on Taylor's philosophy.

Source: http://in.geocities.com/kstability/learning/management/evolution2.html

Scientific management theory and classical organisational theory formed the basis of classical management theory, which concentrated on how to make organisations and their workers operate more efficiently and productively through an analysis of the structure of the organisation.

C.   Administrative Management - Henri Fayol

Henri Fayol, a French engineer and director of mines, was little unknown outside France until the late 40s when Constance Storrs published her translation of Fayol's 1916 " *Administration Industrielle et Generale*".

Fayol's career began as a mining engineer. He then moved into research geology and in 1888 joined Comambault as Director. Comambault was in difficulty but Fayol turned the operation round. On retirement he published his work - a comprehensive theory of administration - described and classified administrative management roles and processes, then became recognised and referenced by others in the growing discourse about management. He is frequently seen as a key early contributor to a classical or administrative management school of thought (even though he himself would never have recognised such a "school").

His theorising about administration was built on personal observation and experience of what worked well in terms of organisation. His aspiration for an "administrative science" sought a consistent set of principles that all organisations must apply in order to run properly.

FW Taylor published *"The Principles of Scientific Management"* in the USA in 1911, and Fayol in 1916 examined the nature of management and administration on the basis of his French mining organisation experiences.

Fayol synthesised various tenets or principles of organisation and management and Taylor on work methods, measurement and simplification to secure efficiencies. Both referenced functional specialisation.

Both Fayol and Taylor were arguing that principles existed which all organisations - in order to operate and be administered efficiently - could implement. This type of assertion typifies a "one best way" approach to management thinking. Fayol's five functions are still relevant to discussion today about management roles and action.

I. **To forecast and plan - purveyance** examine the future and draw up plans of action

II. **To organise -** build up the structure, material and human of the undertaking

III. **To command -** maintain activity among the personnel

IV. **To co-ordinate -** bind together, unify and harmonise activity and effort

V. **To control -** see that everything occurs in conformity with policy and practice

Fayol also synthesised 14 principles for organisational design and effective administration. It is worthwhile reflecting on these and comparing the conclusions to contemporary utterances by Peters, Kanter and Handy to name but three management gurus.

Fayol's 14 principles are:

1. **Specialisation/division of labour**

   A principle of work allocation and specialisation in order to concentrate activities to enable specialisation of skills and understandings, more work focus and efficiency.

2. **Authority with corresponding responsibility**

   If responsibilities are allocated then the post holder needs the requisite authority to carry these out including the right to require others in the area of responsibility to undertake duties.

3. **Discipline**

   The generalisation about discipline is that discipline is essential for the smooth running of a business and without it - standards, consistency of action, adherence to rules and values - no enterprise could prosper. "in an essence - obedience, application, energy, behaviour and outward marks of respect observed in accordance with standing agreements between firms and its employees" (1916).

4. Unity of command

The idea is that an employee should receive instructions from one superior only. This generalisation still holds - even where we are involved with team and matrix structures which involve reporting to more than one boss - or being accountable to several clients. The basic concern is that tensions and dilemmas arise where we report to two or more bosses. One boss may want X, the other Y and the subordinate is caught between the devil and the deep blue sea.

5. Unity of direction

The unity of command idea of having one head (chief executive, cabinet consensus) with agree purposes and objectives and one plan for a group of activities) is clear.

6. Subordination of individual interest to the general interest

Fayol's line was that one employee's interests or those of one group should not prevail over the organisation as a whole. This would spark a lively debate about who decides what the interests of the organisation as a whole are. Ethical dilemmas and matters of corporate risk and the behaviour of individual "chancers" are involved here. Fayol's work assumes a shared set of values by people in the organisation - a unitarism where the reasons for organisational activities and decisions are in some way neutral and reasonable.

7. Remuneration of staff

"The price of services rendered." (1916) The general principle is that levels of compensation should be "fair" and as far as possible afford satisfaction both to the staff and the firm (in terms of its cost structures and desire for profitability/surplus).

8. Centralisation

Centralisation for Fayol is essential to the organisation and a natural consequence of organising. This issue does not go away even where flatter, devolved organisations occur. Decentralisation - is frequently centralised-decentralisation! The modes of control over the actions and results of devolved organisations are still matters requiring considerable attention.

9. Scalar chain/line of authority

The scalar chain of command of reporting relationships from top executive to the ordinary shop operative or driver needs to be sensible, clear and understood.

10. Order

The level of generalisation becomes difficult with this principle. Basically an organisation "should" provide an orderly place for each individual member - who needs to see how their role fits into the organisation and be able to predict the organisation's behaviour towards them. Thus policies, rules, instructions and actions should be understandable and understood. Orderliness implies steady evolutionary movement rather than wild, anxiety-provoking, unpredictable movement.

11. **Equity**

Equity, fairness and a sense of justice "should" pervade the organisation - in principle and practice.

12. **Stability of tenure**

Time is needed for the employee to adapt to his/her work and perform it effectively. Stability of tenure promotes loyalty to the organisation, its purposes and values.

13. **Initiative**

At all levels of the organisational structure, zeal, enthusiasm and energy are enabled by people having the scope for personal initiative. (Note: Tom Peters' recommendations in respect of employee empowerment.)

14. **Esprit de corps**

Here Fayol emphasises the need for building and maintaining harmony among the work force, team work and sound interpersonal relationships.

In the same way that Alfred P Sloan, the executive head of General Motors, reorganised the company into semi-autonomous divisions in the 1920s, corporations undergoing reorganisation still apply "classical organisation" principles - very much in line with Fayol's recommendations.

Source: http://sol.brunel.ac.uk/~jarvis/bola/competence/fayol.html

D. Behavioural Management

Theorists of behavioural management identified the importance and complexity of human behaviour within organisations. The Hawthorne studies demonstrated that workers were more than mere tools of production.

Hawthorne Studies

The research carried out at the Hawthorne plant of the Western Electric Company during the period 1927-1932 were important in showing that scientific management, a concentration solely on the physical aspects of routines and procedures, was inadequate.

In the most famous part of the research, Elton Mayo (a sociologist from Adelaide but working in Harvard), conducted a series of experiments on the effects on production of various levels of illumination. Six female employees were placed in a separate room from their colleagues with the same production equipment and carried on working as the experimenters varied their working conditions. To the amazement of the researchers (remember this was in the early days of work research), no matter what they did, production went up.

The conclusion was that changes in production had nothing to do with changes in conditions but were due to the fact that the employees were being treated as special people. They were being involved. No longer just workers, they were selected people trying to help the company with production research.

Further research was carried out in the bank wiring room of the same company with a group of 14 men. The discovery here was that the group set its own production targets, had a form of solidarity and that incentives had little impact on production. The Hawthorne studies are taken to be the beginning of the human relations movement in the study of management.

No single study has had such an effect on subsequent management thought and practice. It represented a cataclysmic break with traditional theory. For the first time, man's social and individual nature was seen as important to the functioning of organisations.

After Hawthorne, the human relations movement became something of a fad. Malcolm McNair tried to put it in perspective, saying, "the very avidity with which people ... have seized on the fad of human relations itself suggests the presence of a considerable guilt complex." He went on to argue that business is not primarily about keeping people happy and that friction can have its uses, that "... without friction it is possible to go too far in the direction of sweetness and light, harmony and avoidance of all irritation. The ... emphasis on bringing everyone along can easily lead to a deadly level of mediocrity."

The Hawthorne effect: The mere act of paying attention to people spurs them on to do more work.

Abraham Maslow

Most early psychologists studied people with psychological problems, but Abraham Maslow studied successful people. Maslow decided that almost everyone wants to be happy and loving, but they have particular needs that they must meet before they can act unselfishly.

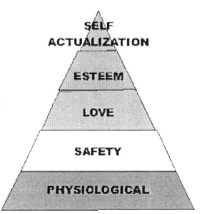

Maslow said that most people want more than they have. Once a person has met their most basic needs, they then develop higher needs. Maslow said, "as one desire is satisfied, another pops up in its place." Maslow created a hierarchy of needs with five levels:

- **Physiological needs.** Biological necessities such as food, water, and oxygen. These needs are the strongest because a person would die if they were not met.

- **Safety needs.** People feel unsafe during emergencies or times of disorder like rioting. Children more commonly have this need met when they feel afraid.

- **Love and belonging needs.** The need to escape loneliness and alienation, to give and receive love, and a sense of belonging.

- **Esteem needs**. The need to feel valuable; to have self-respect and the respect of others. If a person does not fulfil these needs, they feel inferior, weak, helpless, and worthless.

- **Self-actualisation needs**. Maslow taught that a very small group of people reach a level called self-actualisation, where all of their needs are met. Maslow described self-actualisation as a person's finding their "calling." He said, "a musician must make music, an artist must paint, and a poet must write."

Many people confuse self-actualisation with fame or fortune, but often this is not the case. While wealthy or celebrated people might reach self-actualisation, many psychologists believe that most people who have reached the highest level of happiness are unknown beyond their circle of family and friends. Societies develop when people reach a particular level in Maslow's hierarchy. Once people meet their physiological needs and they feel safe, they begin to develop a culture and an advanced civilization.

Douglas McGregor - Theory X and Theory Y

Douglas McGregor in his book *'The Human Side of Enterprise'* published in 1960 has examined theories on behaviour of individuals at work, and he has formulated two models which he calls Theory X and Theory Y.

- **Theory X Assumptions**

The average human being has an inherent dislike of work and will avoid it if he can. Because of their dislike for work, most people must be controlled and threatened before they will work hard enough. The average human prefers to be directed, dislikes responsibility, is unambiguous, and desires security above everything.

These assumptions lie behind most organisational principles today, and give rise both to management with punishments and tight controls, and management that aims at harmony at work.

- **Theory Y Assumptions**

The expenditure of physical and mental effort in work is as natural as play or rest. Control and punishment are not the only ways to make people work, man will direct himself if he is committed to the aims of the organisation. If a job is satisfying, then the result will be commitment to the organisation. The average person learns, under proper conditions, not only to accept but to seek responsibility.

Imagination, creativity, and ingenuity can be used to solve work problems by a large number of employees. Under the conditions of modern industrial life, the intellectual potentialities of the average person are only partially utilised.

- **Comments on Theory X and Theory Y Assumptions**

These assumptions are based on social science research which has been carried out, and demonstrate the potential which is present in a person and which organisations should recognise in order to become more effective. McGregor sees these two theories as two extreme attitudes. Theory Y is difficult to put into practice on the shop floor in large mass production operations, but it can be used initially in the managing of managers and professionals.

In '*The Human Side of Enterprise*' McGregor shows how Theory Y affects the management of promotions and salaries and the development of effective managers. McGregor also sees Theory Y as conducive to participative problem solving. It is part of the manager's job to exercise authority, and there are cases in which this is the only method of achieving the desired results because subordinates do not agree that the ends are desirable.

However, in situations where it is possible to obtain commitment to objectives, it is better to explain the matter fully so that employees grasp the purpose of an action. They will then exert self-direction and control to do better work - quite possibly by better methods - than if they had simply been carrying out an order which they did not fully understand

The situation in which employees can be consulted is one where the individuals are emotionally mature, and positively motivated towards their work; where the work is sufficiently responsible to allow for flexibility and where the employee can see his own position in the management hierarchy. If these conditions are present, managers will find that the participative approach to problem solving leads to much improved results compared with the alternative approach of handing out authoritarian orders. Once management becomes persuaded that it is under-estimating the potential of its human resources, and accepts the knowledge given by social science researchers and displayed in Theory Y assumptions, then it can invest time, money and effort in developing improved applications of the theory. McGregor realises that some of the theories he has put forward are unrealisable in practice, but wants managers to put into operation the basic assumption that staff will contribute more to the organisation if they are treated as responsible and valued employees.

E.   *Contingency Management*

The contingency management approach integrates earlier theories, and suggests that there is no one best way to solve management problems.   A manager's response to a particular problem should depend on the situation.

- Assume there is no one best way to manage.
- The environment impacts the organisation and managers must be flexible to react to environmental changes.
- The way the organisation is designed, control systems selected, depends on the environment.
- Technological environments change rapidly, so must managers.

Henri Mintzberg presents a picture of an all-consuming role for managers and prescriptions about how to behave or techniques to use should be treated with caution.

His conclusions, although related to senior management, seem to reflect the demanding job roles of the mid-1990s - the post-In Search of Excellence, matrix management, lean and down-sized organisation era.

A Realistic Description of Managerial Work?

Henri Mintzberg concluded that:

1. Senior management jobs are open-ended, managers feel compelled to tackle a large workload at demanding pace. There is little free time. Breaks are rare. Escaping from work after hours is physically/mentally difficult.

2. The work is fragmented, full of brevity and variety with a lack of pattern. Managers confront the law of the trivial many and the important few (80/20 principle). Behaviours must change quickly and frequently; interruptions are common.

3. Managers seem to prefer this and become conditioned by workload. Opportunity-costs of time (urgencies) are keenly felt and superficiality in relationships is a hazard.

4. There is an activity-trap - managers tend towards current, specific, well-defined, non-routine activities. Processing mail is a pain; 'non-active' mail gets little attention. Current information (chat, speculation) is preferred - routine reports are not. Use of time reflects close, immediate pressures rather than future, broader issues. Fire-fighting (reacting to immediate stimulus) is a problem. Live action pushes the manager away from thinking and planning.

5. Verbal contacts and media are preferred over written. Written communications get cursory treatment, but must be processed regularly. Less goes out than comes in. It moves slowly. There are long feedback delays. (How does email fit in?) Subordinates outside spoken lines of contact may feel uninformed.

   Informal media (telephone and unscheduled meetings) are used for brief contacts if people know each other well and when quick information exchange is called for.

6. Scheduled meetings eat up managerial time - long formal duration, large groups and often away from the organisation. The agendas cover ceremonials, strategy-making and negotiation. Chatting at start/end of meetings contributes significantly to information flow.

7. Managers seldom 'tour' yet WTJ (walking the job) enhances 'visibility' and understanding of the actuality of work and production/service methods, standards and problems.

8. Managers as boundary managers, link his/her own organisation with outside networks. External contacts (clients, suppliers, associates, peers, informer networks) can consume 30-50% of a senior manager's time. Non-line relationships are also important. Subordinates (line-relationships) consume 30-50% of contact time dealing with requests, information exchanges, making strategy. Open access with subordinates by-passes formal channels. Yet a subordinate spends relatively little time with his/her own superior (10%).

This blend suggested to Mintzberg that managers control little of what they do. Self-control over their initial commitments enables them to unlock the activity trap and orientate themselves to

- extracting information
- exercising leadership

Seminar Questions

A. How does this compare with your current job? Your boss's job? What fine tuning is suggested for your own behaviour as a manager?

B. How can you assist your boss better - if this is the real nature of managerial work?

C. What are the implications for manager training and development?

D. How does information technology-based communication assist such managers - how may IT make matters worse?

Source:http://www.business.com/directory/management/management_theory/conti ngency_and_system_theory/mintzberg%2C_henry

Reading: Bartol, Chapter 2, *Pioneering Ideas in Management.*

Activity

How has a manager's attitude to the workers changed from Classical Management through to Contingency Management? What impact do you think that changing type of work (Less physical/manual more service work), rising skill/education levels, different society expectations of work had on the new theories in management?

_____

_____

_____

_____

_____

_____

Historical perspectives on the role of managers

Fayol (1949)	Mintzberg (1975)	Kotter (1982)	Luthans et al. (1988)	Hill (1992)
Planning	Figurehead	Setting goals and strategies	Exchanging information	**Team leader**
Organising	Leader	Allocating resources	Handling paperwork	**Sales Leader**
Command	Liaison	Monitoring activities	Planning	**Boss**
Coordination	Monitor	Getting information, cooperation and support from superiors	Decision-making	**Supervisor**
Control	Disseminator	Getting cooperation from other groups	Controlling	**Organiser**
	Spokesperson	Motivating, controlling and managing conflict	Interacting with outsiders	**Liaison**
	Entrepreneur		Socialising/ politicking	**Politician**
	Disturbance handler		People manager Motivate/reinforce	
	Resource allocator			**Negotiator**
	Negotiator		Managing conflict	

Task Force Research: Callan Consulting 1995

Source: Karpin Report: Executive Summary April 1995. AGPS

Activity

As a manager, describe how your role has changed and how you think it will change in the future.

_____

_____

_____

_____

'Old' and 'new' paradigms of management

New Paradigm	Old Paradigm
organisation learning	organisation discipline
virtuous circles	vicious circles
flexible organisations	inflexible organisations
management leaders	management administrators
open communication	distorted communication
markets	hierarchies
product development driven by core competencies	product development driven by strategic business units
strategic learning capacities are widespread	strategic learning occurs at the apex of the organisation
assumption that most employees are trustworthy	assumption that most employees are untrustworthy
most employees are empowered	most employees are disempowered
local knowledge of all employees is critical to success and creativity creates its own prerogative	local knowledge of all employees must be disciplined by managerial prerogative

Task Force Research: University of Western Sydney, 1995

What a manager is expected to do has changes as the organisation and the expectations of what staff expect from their employer has changed. These changes are likely to continue.

Trends perceived to have the most significant impact on managers in the future

Table IV
Managers' views of the skills they will require in the next five years

	All	1-50	51-500	501-5,000	More than 5,000
Using IT	61.4	62.4	65.4	61.4	56.8
Managing information/knowledge	41.9	43.1	34.6	40.0	49.5
Financial management	38.5	36.6	35.0	38.3	43.9
Strategic thinking	35.3	30.7	34.3	39.3	36.9
Project management	29.4	22.4	22.6	33.1	38.9
Communication skills	25.9	29.0	21.6	29.3	23.9
Leadership/motivational skills	24.3	23.1	22.3	24.8	26.9
Marketing skills	24.3	33.4	22.6	19.7	21.6
Negotiating	22.9	20.0	24.0	23.4	23.9
Environmental management	22.1	19.0	28.6	22.4	18.6
Coaching and counselling	20.9	17.6	23.0	22.4	20.6
Foreign languages	20.4	21.0	23.3	18.6	18.9
Interpersonal skills	16.9	15.9	11.3	20.7	19.6
Working as part of team	9.7	6.9	8.5	10.3	13.0

Sources: Les Worrall, Cary Cooper Management skills development: a perspective on current issues and setting the future agenda Leadership & Organisation Development Journal Volume 22 Number 1 2001 pp. 34-39

Management theory has developed over time in response to changes that have occurred in the type of work performed, the changing expectations of employees and customers, changes in skills and knowledge of workers, the changing technology and the structure of business. Managing an organisation now is far more complex and the changes facing organisations are occurring more quickly and from a wider range of sources that managers need to develop skills in assessing their external environment in order to predict their future.

This course is designed to provide you with the academic framework to analyse your organisation's environment and the interface between your organisation and this environment. This course is the first step in the process of understanding the future changes in your environment so that you can use this knowledge to develop and implement strategies that will allow you to survive in the future. In this course we are adopting a '**systems theory**' approach to understanding an organisation and its environment.

Systems Theory

Managers have been urged to think of organisations as **living systems** that are defined by a complex set of internal and external relationships and connections of ideas.

> "The perception of the organisation as a machine or physical entity is a death warrant for organisations. We need to alter our perceptions before we begin to work with people to undertake the process of transformation now required for success.
>
> The organisation is a self regulating and adaptive systems. Unlike 'physical' or mechanical systems such as computer circuits, plumbing, wiring, or heating, organisations and other living systems constantly change within themselves as a result of stimulation from their environment."

> *Source: Clancy, David and Weber, Robert Chapter 1 'Roses and Rust: redefining the essence of leadership in a new age' Sydney: Business and Professional Publishing 1995*

Organisations can be viewed as a number of interrelated sub-systems (Kast and Rosenzweig) within their environments. This concept is based on the biological and physical sciences. The system has inputs, transformation processes, outputs or products and feedback. The focus is on the organisation as a whole and the interrelationships of structure and behaviour within the organisation. This "systems theory" introduces the concept of 'open' and 'closed' management systems.

The survival of an organisation is dependent on effective exchanges between:

- Individuals and their organisation
- The organisation and its environment

If the first of these does not exist then there will be low morale, labour unrest, high turnover and absenteeism.

If the second does not exist, then the organisation does not respond to the changes occurring in its environment, over time it will no longer meet the needs in the market place (it becomes ineffective).

Figure: System Theory

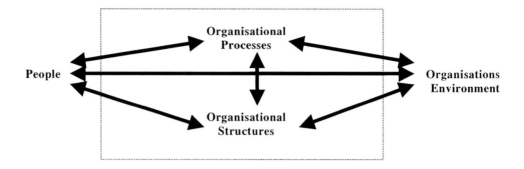

A **system** is not just a collection of parts.

"A system is a set of interacting units or elements that form an integrated whole intended to perform some function".

Skyttner Lars 'General systems theory: origin and hallmarks', Kybernetes, Vol. 25, No 6, 1996 pp 16-22 © MCB University Press.

"A system is an entity that maintains its existence and functions as a whole through the interaction of its parts."

O'Connor, J. and McDermott, I. (1997). Chapter 1 'What is a system?' In The art of systems thinking. London : Thorsons, pp 2–25.

A System	A Heap
Interconnecting parts functioning as a whole.	A collection of parts.
Changes if you take away pieces or add more pieces. If you cut a system in half, you do not get two smaller systems, but a damaged system that will probably not function.	Essential properties are unchanged whether you add or take away pieces. When you halve a heap, you get two smaller heaps.
The arrangement of the pieces is crucial.	The arrangement of the pieces is irrelevant.
The parts are connected and work together.	The parts are not connected and can function separately.
Its behaviour depends on the total structure. Change the structure and the behaviour changes.	Its behaviour (if any) depends on its size or the number of pieces in the heap.

An **open system** is one in which the organisation interacts with its external environment and is in turn influenced by it. Information and impacts from the outside world cross the interface between the organisation and outside environment, influencing internal relationships and operations. Feedback occurs also with the organisation continually adjusting to the various environmental and organisational sub systems. The whole system is greater than the sum of its parts (synergy).

Considers relationships inside and outside the organisation.

The environment consists of forces, conditions, and influences outside the organisation.

Systems theory also considers the impact of stages:

> **Input:** acquire external resources.

> **Conversions:** inputs are processed into goods and services.

> **Output:** finished goods are released into the environment.

In contrast, the Classical and human relations approaches generally view organisations as closed systems as they assume that control of internal matters is sufficient to manage the organisation.

The environments of an organisation include the social, political, technological and economic forces that affect it. Managers should not be surprised if the success of a new product release is affected by such things as: interest rates, government policy, and consumer preference impact on the environments. This aspect will be dealt with in more detail later in the course.

As contemporary managers you need to recognise the open nature of systems. When solving problems, managers must take into account the impact of their decisions on stakeholders of the organisation. Stakeholders include employees, customers, and community groups.

Under this approach there are implications for planning (eg need for integration between departments and sections) coordination and control, HRM (eg team building) and so on.

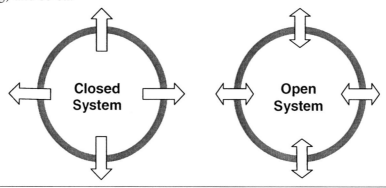

Open and Closed Systems

An **open system** interacts with the environment. A **closed system** is self-contained.

A closed system often undergoes entropy and loses the ability to control itself, and fails.

Synergy: performance gains of the whole surpass the components.

Synergy is only possible in a coordinated system.

It is the **emergent properties** that give a system life. Emergent properties are those functions, attributes or behaviours, good or bad, that would not exist except for the operation of the system. It is both the nature of the elements and the interrelationships that give rise to emergent properties

---

Systems thinking is:

❖ Paying attention to relationships and not parts. What something does and how important it is depends on how it fits with other parts. The properties of a system are the properties of the whole.

❖ Looking beyond isolated events to deeper patterns. When you understand how the system is made up, its structure, then you can influence and predict events and not be at their mercy.

❖ Thinking in circles of mutual influence not straight lines of cause/effect/stop. What you do has effects that come back to influence what you do next.

❖ Appreciating the big picture as well as the parts. Seeing both the wood, and the trees. Recognising that at one level everything is related and you define the boundaries of any system you deal with.

Advantages of Systems Management

There are a number of benefits of thinking of organisations as systems:

1. Systems awareness provides a way of thinking about management that allows managers to take into account the tremendous amount of knowledge and information available to them.

2. Systems thinking provides the manager with a frame of reference by which the manager can relate one subsystem or work specialty with another or with others.

3. Systems concepts help the manager raise his or her sights above the day to day routine of current in-house operations and understand how his or her responsibilities relate to the total organisation and how the total organisation relates to the superordinate systems in the environment.

Summary

The system approach has limits as it can be abstract and it does not explain all that goes on in an organisation. However, it is useful in that it adds to the knowledge and understanding of organisations and organisation theory especially in relation to the concepts of interdependency and environmental linkages.

Using the systems approach allows you to consider the change that occurs in interaction between subgroups within the organisation as well as the changes with in the work group.

Complexity

A system maintains itself through the interaction of its parts, and so it is the relationships and the mutual influence between the parts that is important rather than the number or size of the parts.

The complexity in a system is not in the number of separate bits involved but in the many different ways that the parts can be put together or related to each other (dynamic complexity).

The simplest systems will have a few parts that have only a few states with a few simple relationships between those parts (ie a plumbing system).

A very complex system may have parts or subsystems, all of which can have different states, which may change in response to other parts.

Organisational Responses to Complexity

Complexity theory suggests that because organisations are complex adaptive systems, those which:

- perceive turbulent and complex environments which develop *complexity absorption* managerial responses will be more successful than those which develop *complexity reduction* managerial responses to their environments.

- encourage, recognise and enhance new connections are more capable of co-evolving effectively with their environment

Definitions

Complexity Reduction – organisations simplify their internal make-up as a way of achieving order in what seems like a disorderly world:

- good managers are those who achieve stability and balance in a system

- organisations find it difficulty to break away from an emphasis on over-learned behaviour because of the firm's dominant logic

- organisations seem to move towards simpler/narrower interpretations of the world

- impose order and attempt to eliminate ambiguity.

Complexity Absorption – organisations develop multiple, sometimes conflicting goals and structural flexibility:

- recognition of a variety of strategic alternatives

- more decentralised structural decision-making patterns

- pursuit of a wide variety of interactions and connections for decision making.

- acceptance of ambiguity and disorder.

Complexity Absorption Responses[1]

1. Goal Complexity

Achieved when organisations pursue many different kinds of goals (eg pursuit of multiple goals with portfolio strategies).

2. Strategic Complexity

Achieved when the organisation simultaneously pursues a variety of strategic objectives (eg quality and cost leadership).

3. Interaction Complexity

Achieved when there are high levels of participation by multiple groups in strategic direction-making (ie high levels of participation allow richer more detailed observation of strategic events rather than lower levels of participation by fewer internal stakeholders.

4. Structural Complexity

Achieved when there is greater internal variety in the organisation (ie.more decentralised, less formalised organisations).

Viewpoint

"Organisations that respond managerially to environmental turbulence and complexity with absorption responses (ie internal goal complexity, strategic complexity, interaction complexity and structural complexity) outperform organisations that pursue complexity reduction responses."[2]

---

[1] Source: Ashmos D. & Duchon D. (2000) *'Organisational responses to complexity: the effect on organisational performance'*, Journal of Organisational Change Management, Vol 13, No 6.

[2] Source: J Jepson/J Luker Strategic Concepts.

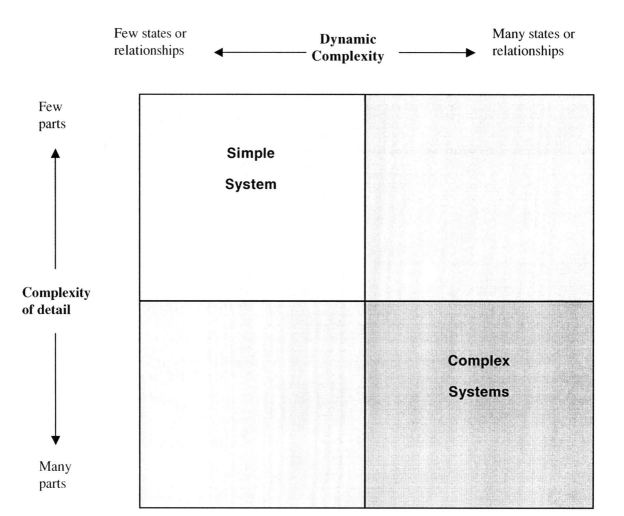

Order
Total Integration
Total Cooperation

Complexity
Integration-Differentiation
Cooperation-Competition

Numerous interactions, enough of them with positive feedback,
Lead to self-organising behaviour of complex systems

Chaos
Total Differentiation
Total Competition

Figure: Evolving systems are complex[3]

[3] Journal of Knowledge Management Vol. 2, pg. 60, 2 December 1998.

Organisational Systems

These days, a different ideal for organisations is surfacing. We want organisations to be adaptive, flexible, self-renewing, resilient, learning, intelligent-attributes found only in living systems. The tension of our times is that we want our organisations to behave as living systems, but we only now know to treat them as machines.

Systems thinking as managers[4]

We all know that managers should look at the big picture. But the actual skills whereby managers are supposed to achieve this are not well understood. Successful managers often are 'systems thinkers' to a considerable extent. Their focus is less on day-to-day events and more on underlying trends and forces of change. But they do this almost completely intuitively. The consequence is that they are often unable to explain their intuitions to others and feel frustrated that others cannot see the work the way they do.

Suggestions as to what system thinking makes more effective managers by:

❖ *Seeing interrelationships, not things, and processes, not snapshots.* Most of us have been conditioned throughout our lives to focus on things and to see the world in static images. This leads us to linear explanations of systemic phenomenon.

❖ *Moving beyond blame.* We tend to blame each other or outside circumstances for our problems. It is poorly designed systems, not incompetent or unmotivated individuals, which cause most organisational problems. Systems' thinking shows us that there is not outside – that you and the cause of your problems are part of a single system.

❖ *Distinguishing detail complexity from dynamic complexity.* Some types of complexity are more important strategically than others. Complexity arises when there are many variables. It is not about knowing the details of the system that is important, it is about knowing those elements which are significant and those whose causes and effects that are of importance, (dynamic complexity)

❖ *Focusing on areas of high importance.* Systems thinking shows that small, well-focused actions can produce significant, enduring improvements, if they are in the right place. Systems thinkers refer to this idea as the principle of leverage. Tackling a difficult problem is often a matter of seeing where the high leverage lies, where a change – with a minimum of effort – would lead to lasting, significant improvement.

---

4 Bob de Wit and Ron Meyer 'Strategy – Process, content, context ' 2nd edition International Thomson Business Press 1998.

❖ *Avoiding symptomatic solutions.* The pressures to intervene in management systems that are going awry can be overwhelming. Unfortunately, given the linear thinking that predominates in most organisations, interventions usually focus on symptomatic fixes, not underlying causes. This results in only temporary relief, and it tends to create still more pressures later on for further, low-leverage intervention. If leaders acquiesce to these pressures, they can be sucked into an endless spiral of increasing intervention. Sometimes the most difficult leadership acts are to refrain from intervening through popular quick fixes and to keep the pressure on everyone to identify more enduring solutions.

Activity

Answer the following questions.

1. How does the concept of organisations as systems apply to your organisation?

2. Are you operating in an open or closed system?

3. Do they fit into the Complexity Absorption or the Complexity reduction camp?

4. How does system-thinking assist the way we think about organisations' design?

UNIT 2

ORGANISATIONS' MISSIONS/VISIONS

Traditional Approach to Strategic Planning

Most organisations will do some form of formal strategic planning that involves creating a corporate Mission and Vision for the organisation, developing corporate objectives and strategies. This is intended to set the overall purpose and direction for the organisation. As middle/lower level managers you are required to recognise and use these documents to set your unit's strategies and budgets.

This Unit will describe the corporate planning process and then look at how you in your role as managers contribute to this strategic direction.

The Mission

The Mission is the intent, spirit or rally cry which constitutes the organisation's and its members' primary duty or way of behaving - the foundation and force which throws, sends, or casts itself into the future towards its goals and targets.

Benefits

A clear, concise mission statement has the following benefits:

- It is an enduring statement of purpose and of the reason the business exists.

- It provides an important focus and screen for the selection of appropriate strategies and functional objectives.

- It helps maintain consistency and unanimity of purpose throughout the enterprise. Employees know the values that the business strives to maintain.

- It serves as a reminder of performance and provides motivation for the maintenance of those standards.

Purpose

- It provides a focus for the diverse sections of the organisation so that they are all 'pulling' in the same direction.

- It maintains consistency of purpose and performance standards.

- It contributes to motivation within the organisation.

> **Example**
>
> We fulfil dreams through the experience of motorcycling, by providing to motorcyclists and to the general public an expanding line of motorcycles and branded products and services in selected market segments.
>
> *Harley Davidson – Company Mission*

The Vision

The Vision conceptualises something seen which is not actually present or historical, something which may be a notion of the future that can provide something to anticipate and aim towards or away from (like your old school motto).

Benefits

A vision:

- enhances a wide range of performance measures
- promotes change
- provides the basis for the strategic plan
- motivates individuals and facilitates the recruitment of talent
- helps keep decision making in context.

Source: Lipton, Mark Sloan, Management Review, Summer 1996 p83.

Strategic Intent

To assist in focusing attention on what the organisation is concentrating on in the shorter term, organisations may also or instead of the complex missions and visions issue Strategic Intent statements, eg 'To beat Coca Cola', 'To be the best in Black and White'.

The corporate mission plays three important roles for a business organisation. The roles are:

1. *Direction.*

   The corporate mission can point the organisation in a certain direction, by defining the boundaries within which strategic choices and action must take place. By specifying the fundamental principles on which strategies must be based, the corporate mission limits the scope of strategic options and sets the organisation on a particular heading.

2. *Legitimisation.*

   The corporate mission can convey to all stakeholders inside and outside the company that the organisation is pursuing valuable activities in a proper way. By specifying the business philosophy that will guide the company, it is hoped that stakeholders will accept, support and trust the organisation.

3. *Motivation.*

   The corporate mission can go a step further than legitimisation, by actually inspiring individuals to work together in a particular way. By specifying the fundamental principles driving organisational actions, an *espirit de corps* can evolve, with the powerful capacity to motivate people over a prolonged period of time.

   Source: DeWit B. and Meyer R. (1998), Strategy: Process, Content, Context, International Thomson, London p 812.

Corporate goals and objectives

Corporate goals describe what the organisation wants to achieve. They are usually destinations the organisation is aiming for in the long term.

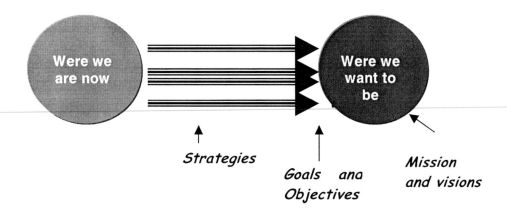

Corporate Objectives is a precise result that the organisation wishes to reach in a given time frame. They tend to be more specific and short term than goals.

Objectives are usually set in conjunction with lower level management so that they have the following characteristics:

- **Clear:** can be understood by those to whom it applies
- **Realistic:** achievable, otherwise it will be ignored or it will de-motive employees.
- **Measurable:** how well they have been achieved can be determined.
- **Attainable within a time limit:** when are they expected to be achieved.

Corporate strategies

Typically when people refer to an organisation's strategy they are talking about the whole pattern of decisions that sets the long-term direction of the organisation.

Strategies are usually characterised by:

- A concern with consistency; or the coherence of a pattern over time. They are about several years' commitment of resources, all resources pushing the organisation in the same direction.
- A commitment of major resources, whether these resources be financial, material or human
- The irrevocable nature of the decisions attributed to the strategy. This means that if you spend money on, for example, staff training to achieve a goal then if the strategy and goal changes, the training and the money spent is wasted.

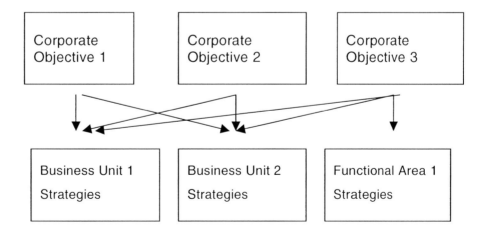

Goal	Objective
To encourage and reward employee contributions and participation.	To nominate at least one employee from my department for the biannual Customer Service Hero Award and to win this award at least once every two years.
To build the most reliable and environmentally sound vehicle batteries in New Zealand.	To have a pass rate at final test stage of, or better than, 99.5% by June 2003.
To be the largest retailer of passenger tyres in Australia.	To have 25% market share as measured by our total sales and to have 3% more stores than our nearest competitorby February 2005

Source : Cole Kris 'Supervision' 2nd ed 2001 Prentice Hall ISBN 1 74009 292 9 p 161.

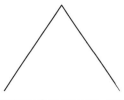

CORPORATE PLANS

- Mission/Vision
- Competitive Position
- Resource Development/Allocation

BUSINESS UNIT PLANS

- How to compete in a particular market
- How to achieve corporate objectives in that area

OPERATIONAL/FUNCTIONAL PLANS
- Budgets and action plans for area

Levels of planning

Corporate planning tends to be top down. Senior managers undertake the corporate planning process whether formally (strategic planning) or informally (strategic thinking) along the lines provided in the following diagram.

Mission and visions and corporate planning are for the long term; depending on the organisation they may stay in place for five to ten years. Increasingly however we are seeing then being refined as the environment the organisation faces becomes more turbulent or a new Chief Executive wants to initiate a new era.

Three Levels Of Planning[1]

Responsibilities		Time spent on planning	Time horizons
Corporate and strategic plan	Top Management		10 years
Long-term survival Future profits	Chief executive	67%	
Future resources Functional division plans	President, Vice-president General managers Divisional managers (SBUs) (Proactive – high risk takers)	48%	
Implementation of operations program	Middle Management		2 years
Operating Problems Present profits Plan and allocate resources	Divisional managers, product line and functional managers, department managers, plant managers (Conservative, reactive, problem solvers)	63%	6 months
Develop programs to effectively and efficiently utilise resources	Lower Management Functional managers, unit managers, supervisors, forepersons (conservative, reactive)	78%	6 months 1 week

1 Adapted from: F.R. David (1989) Concepts of Strategic Management, Columbus, Ohio: Merrill, p169, R.M. Hodgetts (1985) Management: International Edition, US: Academic Press, pp90-91; L.N. Redman (1983) 'The Planning Process', Managerial Planning, 31, p28, J.A.F. Stoner, R.R. Collins and P.W. Yetton (1985) Management in Australia, Sydney: Prentice Hall, pp121, 154.

The Strategic Management Process

Strategy Formulation

Strategy Implementation

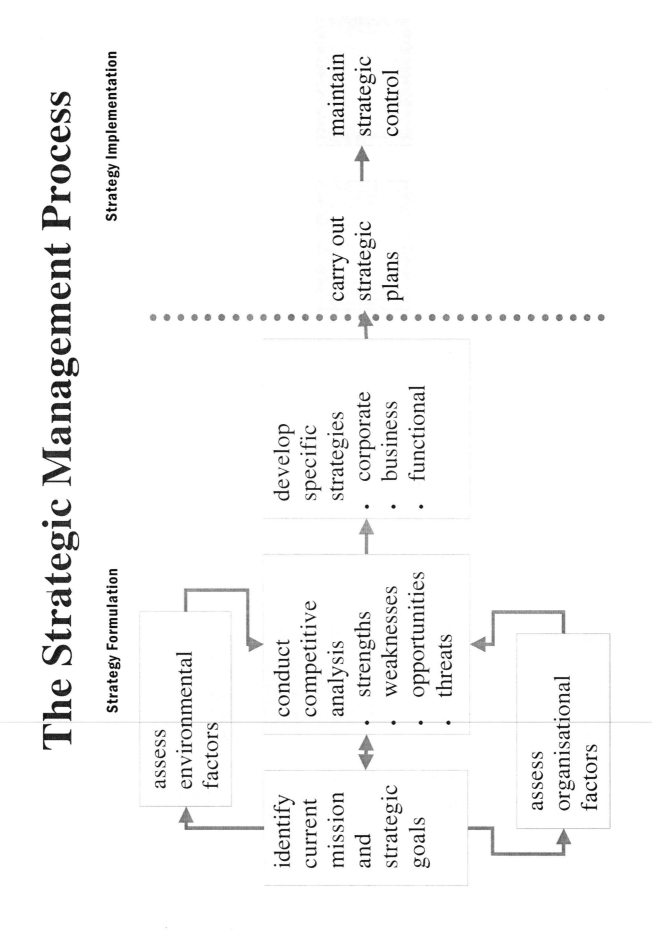

assess
environmental
factors

identify
current
mission
and
strategic
goals

assess
organisational
factors

conduct
competitive
analysis

- strengths
- weaknesses
- opportunities
- threats

develop
specific
strategies

- corporate
- business
- functional

carry out
strategic
plans

maintain
strategic
control

Three Primary Levels Of Management

Senior Management

- Define mission, values, and vision
- Set strategic objectives and initiate significant shifts in the direction of the enterprise
- Monitor corporate and group results
- Obtain and broadly allocate capital resources
- Maintain relations with key external parties, including shareholders, key customers, public
- Ensure availability of senior management talent
- Determine the overall management organisation structure
- Provide the philosophy and example on "how we manage"

Middle Management

- Set operational performance objectives for each unit
- Allocate resources needed for performance
- Exchange information with other management levels and units
- Participate in key customer relations and account decisions
- Develop key management and professional talent

First-Level Management

- Set employee performance activities, objectives, standards
- Provide training, coaching, resources to support performance
- Give employees feedback on performance
- Provide recognitions, rewards, and incentives
- Ensure that business practices are consistent with desired values
- Maintain contact with key customers.

Middle/Lower Level Management

The role of lower level management is to adopt the Missions/Visions and Strategic intent in their business unit or functional planning. The unit then will operate in sync with the rest of the organisation. The alternative is that the unit or functional area will develop independently and not to the benefit of the whole organisation. Your unit may become very efficient at what it is doing but it may be doing the wrong things in terms of the organisation and its customers (being ineffective).

As managers you need not only to understand the mission, visions and strategic intent, but also to understand how these goals and objectives relate to your business unit or functional area.

The goals and objectives become the framework for planning within your unit or functional area.

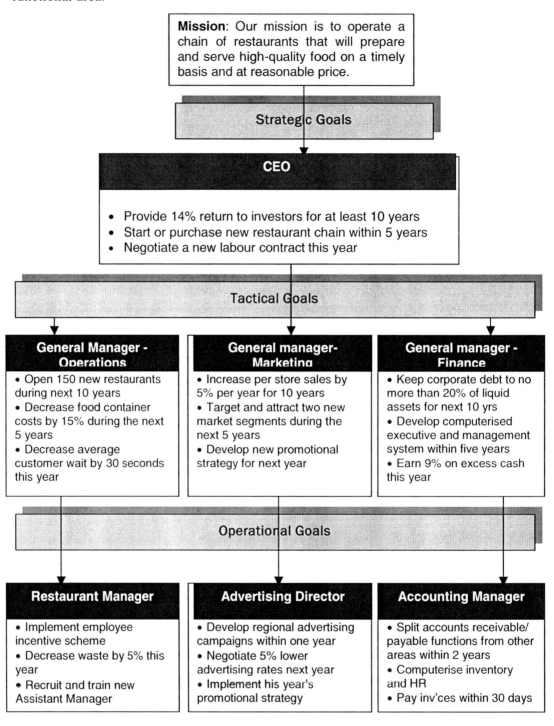

Mission: Our mission is to operate a chain of restaurants that will prepare and serve high-quality food on a timely basis and at reasonable price.

Strategic Goals

CEO

- Provide 14% return to investors for at least 10 years
- Start or purchase new restaurant chain within 5 years
- Negotiate a new labour contract this year

Tactical Goals

General Manager - Operations
- Open 150 new restaurants during next 10 years
- Decrease food container costs by 15% during the next 5 years
- Decrease average customer wait by 30 seconds this year

General manager- Marketing
- Increase per store sales by 5% per year for 10 years
- Target and attract two new market segments during the next 5 years
- Develop new promotional strategy for next year

General manager - Finance
- Keep corporate debt to no more than 20% of liquid assets for next 10 yrs
- Develop computerised executive and management system within five years
- Earn 9% on excess cash this year

Operational Goals

Restaurant Manager
- Implement employee incentive scheme
- Decrease waste by 5% this year
- Recruit and train new Assistant Manager

Advertising Director
- Develop regional advertising campaigns within one year
- Negotiate 5% lower advertising rates next year
- Implement his year's promotional strategy

Accounting Manager
- Split accounts receivable/payable functions from other areas within 2 years
- Computerise inventory and HR
- Pay inv'ces within 30 days

Kinds of organisational goals for a regional fast-food chain from Davidson P. and Griffin R.W. *'Management: An Australasian Perspective'* 2nd ed John Wiley & Sons Australia, Ltd

Organisations develop many different kinds of goals that go down through the organisation to be interpreted and implemented at the operational level.

Units may need to respond and adopt lots of different goals and sometimes they experience conflict or contradictions among goals. Lower cost is usually inconsistent with higher quality, Human resource section may have a conflict between flexible work force or cost control and the need to maintain a motivated work force and retain intellectual knowledge.

Optimising: A process of balancing and reconciling conflicts between goals.

Format for this course

This course is about how you go about contributing to the strategic direction of your organisation by creating appropriate strategies and targets for your functional or business units and how you then manage the process to attain these outcomes.

The manager's task is to create:

- competitive and functional strategies
- targets and performance benchmarks
- how you monitor and control the process

At the completion of this course you will be able to:

- Analyse the external environment
- Understand your unit's competitive position
- Apply the resource based model to your unit
- Develop appropriate business level strategies

In the subject *Develop and Implement Strategic Plans* you will look at how you implement a strategic plan.

Reference: Thompson J.L. (1997) Strategic Management: Awareness and Change, 3rd Ed, Thomson International Business Press.

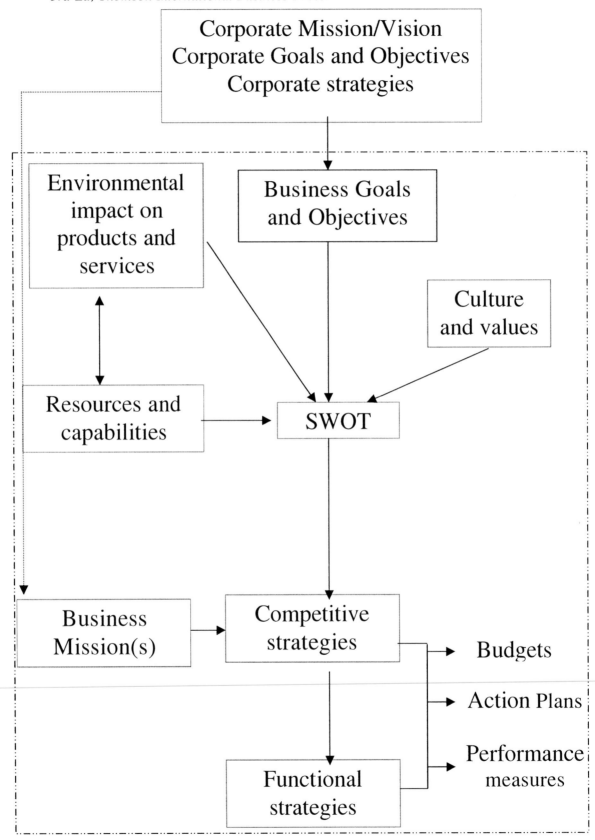

Hierarchy and Definition of Terms

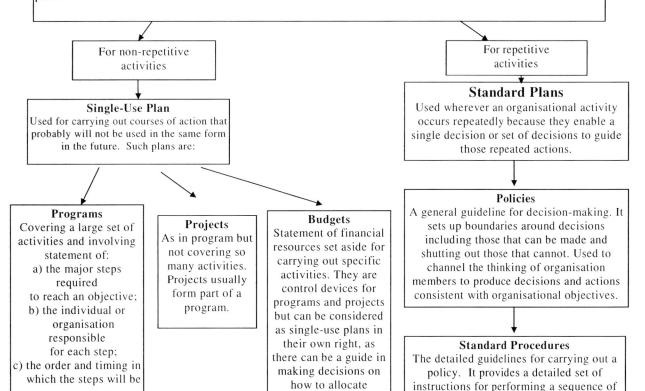

Vision
Conceptualises something seen which is not actually present or historical, something which may be a notion of the future which can provide something to anticipate and aim towards or away from

Mission
Is the intent, spirit or rally cry which constitutes the organisation's and its member's, primary duty or way of behaving, the foundation and force which throws, sends, or casts itself into the future toward its goals and targets.

Objectives/Goals
The ends to be achieved in order to carry out this mission defined in measurable terms in quantity and time.

Strategies & Strategic Plans
Strategies: Broad programs for achieving objectives and thus implementing the mission. They guide deployment of resources that will be used to move the organisation towards its objectives.
Strategic Planning: A plan which defines the objectives of the organisation and the means used to achieve the objectives. It is concerned with the BROAD concept of the organisation in the future and the provision and allocation of priorities and resources.
General Planning: A continuing process for deciding the allocation of priorities and total resources now in order to achieve stated objectives by a given time in the future.
Tactical Planning: Embraces all the detailed plans and actions involved in implementing the strategic plan.

For non-repetitive activities

For repetitive activities

Single-Use Plan
Used for carrying out courses of action that probably will not be used in the same form in the future. Such plans are:

Standard Plans
Used wherever an organisational activity occurs repeatedly because they enable a single decision or set of decisions to guide those repeated actions.

Programs
Covering a large set of activities and involving statement of:
a) the major steps required
to reach an objective;
b) the individual or organisation responsible
for each step;
c) the order and timing in which the steps will be completed.

Projects
As in program but not covering so many activities. Projects usually form part of a program.

Budgets
Statement of financial resources set aside for carrying out specific activities. They are control devices for programs and projects but can be considered as single-use plans in their own right, as there can be a guide in making decisions on how to allocate resources among various alternative activities.

Policies
A general guideline for decision-making. It sets up boundaries around decisions including those that can be made and shutting out those that cannot. Used to channel the thinking of organisation members to produce decisions and actions consistent with organisational objectives.

Standard Procedures
The detailed guidelines for carrying out a policy. It provides a detailed set of instructions for performing a sequence of actions that occurs often or regularly.

Typical Strategic Objectives[2]

Profitability	Attain a 20 percent return on investment within the next two years. Increase net income by $50 million within the next three years.
Market standing	Attain a 30 percent share of the market in less than 5 years from now. Increase non-cosmetics product sales to 60 percent of total.
R & D	Develop at least one patented product every year. Increase the research and development budget by 5 percent a year from the next 5 years.
Financial resource	Decrease long-term debt by $30 million within the next 3 years. Increase working capital to $15 million within the next 4 years.
Human resources	In the next 4 years, put all top management personnel through an executive development program developed in conjunction with a leading business school in the area.
Productivity	Produce at the rate of at least 100 units per hour in the next 2 years.
Physical resources	Increase production capacity by 25 percent within the next 5 years.
Customer Service	Increase the on-time delivery rate to 95 percent before the end of next year.
Social responsibility	Allocate at least 0.5 percent of earnings before income taxes for philanthropy. Donate the time of at least 5 managers per year for teaching in colleges and universities

---

[2] Source: G.Boseman, A.Phatak and R.E. Schellenberger (1986), *Strategic Management: Text and Cases*, NY: Wiley, p. 59.

Activity

Mission Statements

BRL Hardy[3]

Our Vision:

Quality Wines for the World

Our Mission:

We will manage the business to maximise the long term return to shareholders while recognising the importance of customers, employees, suppliers and the community.

We will build world class brands which promote enduring consumer loyalty by continuing to increase quality and consistency.

We will achieve our objectives by sustaining superior performance, by understanding and satisfying customer needs, by encouraging creative production and marketing skills and through providing a stimulating environment in which to work and grow

Burnside War Memorial Hospital4

Mission Statement

The Burnside Hospital provides a range of health care services delivered by a team of highly skilled, professional and compassionate staff who strive to exceed patient and consumer expectations within a safe environment. The contemporary and competitively priced services, provided across a continuum, are of the highest standard and responsive to the needs of the hospital's client community.

Our Values

The key values of respect for the individual, teamwork, and quality are integral to Burnside Hospital's primary goal of achieving excellence in patient care and associated services. We value:

- the rights of our patients, focusing on respect for their privacy, dignity and individual needs;
- the professional association with our visiting medical and allied health staff;
- the opportunity to provide high quality services to patients and consumers

---

[3] About BRL Hardy http://www.brlhardy.com.au/about/main.html accessed 23/09/2002.

[4] Burnside War Memorial Hospital http://burnsidehospital.asn.au/about_us/ms_au.html accessed 18/09/01.

- a workplace where a collegial approach, trust and respect enable individuals to deliver service excellence;
- the responsibility to use available resources effectively and efficiently; and
- the conservation of our natural environment

For these two organisations, use your imagination to set two goals and two objectives for each that are consistent with their missions/visions.

_____

_____

_____

_____

_____

_____

_____

_____

_____

_____

_____

_____

_____

_____

_____

_____

_____

_____

_____

_____

UNIT 3

ANALYSING THE ENVIRONMENT

The previous session described corporate missions and visions and how they relate to the unit's mission/visions, strategies and budgets. This session initiates the process and theory you need understand as managers to develop your units strategies. Initially we will look at how you analyse and understand your environment. We will look at the process of developing strategies from this environmental perspective using Michael Porter's theories.

In later sessions we will look at developing strategies from the internal perspective using the resource based model, which will allow you to understand and develop your units core capabilities.

Types of external environments

This course focuses on the environment in which managers must manage, both inside and outside the company. The point is that managers cannot be arbitrary in their decisions, there are many other circumstances that affect what they can and cannot do, as well as what will or will not work.

Try to broaden your perspective through this course: There is a dual environment in which you exist and work and this course provides a means of examining and describing that environment. Try to build a unified picture of the world around you that you describe using the terms in this course.

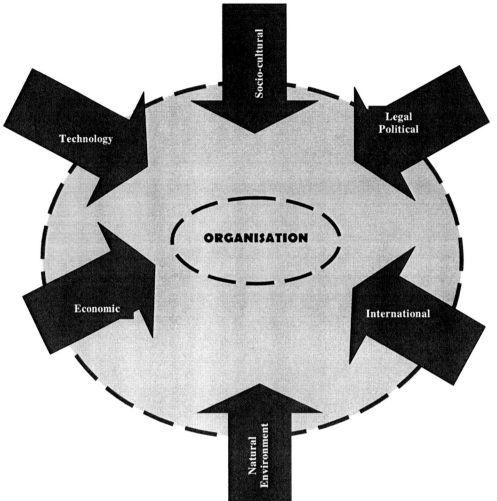

The **mega-environment,** or general environment, is the segment of the **external environment** that reflects the broad conditions and trends in the societies within which an organisation operates. In assessing the general environment of an organisation we are interested in the future not the past. What are the future trends or conditions that are going to impact on the organisation, whether directly or through our competitors or customers?

1. The **technological element** is the part of the general-environment that reflects the current state of knowledge regarding the production of products and services.

    a. Research indicates that technology tends to evolve through periods of incremental change punctuated by technological breakthroughs that either enhance or destroy the competence of firms in an industry.

    b. Shifts in technology.

c.   Australia is now facing technological competition, customer's expectations increase and countries look to develop their technological infrastructure.

2.   The **economic element** is the part of the general-environment that covers the systems of producing, distributing and consuming wealth. The overall health of the economic system in which the organisation operates.

   a.   Organisations are influenced by a variety of economic conditions over which they have little control, such as inflation and interest rates. The stability of the economy is also important - will interest rates remain low, will the economy continue to expand steadily? Are there different sectors where customer demand is higher or lower? For example we have seen the home building industry continue to perform well, in part due to the continued assistance provided to first home owners.

   The change in prices (inflation) does not occur evenly over all sectors of the economy. The price of property in the mid 1980s rose faster than the general change in prices.

   b.   The cyclical nature of the economic cycle impact on the industries and organisations. Business cycles, boom and recession as the economy periodically expands and then contracts. Stock market cycles of 'bulls' and 'bears' when the stock market indices either climbs or slides down in value.

   c.   Unemployment levels in the state/nationally. These are usually seasonally adjusted to allow for the fluctuations as school leavers enter the market. The unemployment in different sectors of the economy we are seeking certain categories of higher than average unemployment for example among the youth, over 50 year olds, low skilled workers.

   d.   The rise of the knowledge economics.

3.   The **legal-political element** is the part of the general environment that includes the legal and governmental systems within which an organisation must function.

   a.   Organisations must operate within the general legal framework of the countries in which they do business, eg accounting rules and legal processes. How your accounting systems are set up are determined by the Accounting bodies, the Australian Securities Commission, the Taxation Dept, etc.

Accounting standards

Accounting Standards establish the procedures on how to account for certain transactions and events, as well as providing detail disclosure requirements.

All Accounting Standards are set by the AASB (Australian Accounting Standards Board)

According to corporation's law, compliance with the Accounting Standards issued by the AASB is mandatory for all companies that are reporting entities. Other jurisdictions such as state governments may also adopt AASB standards and make compliance with such standards mandatory. The Australian Securities and Investments Commission (ASIC) is responsible for enforcing compliance with Corporations Law

The major accounting organisations in Australia are: Australian Society of CPA's, Institute of Chartered Accountants, and the National Institute of Accountants.

The Australian Society of CPA's and the Chartered Institute of Accountants are the two major associations in Australia that develop the rules and practices for the accounting profession. These standards are **compulsory for all members of the accounting profession.**

---

b.   Legislation and the outcome of court cases determines what legal rules organisations need to abide by. The clean air and clean water acts, OH&S and EEO. These do not stay static over time amendments and new interpretations (precedents) in the court room. Precedents by barristers in an argument and by judges in the course of handing down their decisions are a way of taking advantage of the experience and wisdom of others. The system of reporting court cases and the use of precedent means that the legal rules and regulations are a fluid and open system. The organisation needs to monitor how the system changes impacts on the way it operates. For example what is impact of the latest court decision on unfair dismissal?

c.   We are also in an increasingly litigious country as we follow the trends in the USA. Organisations are subject to an increase in lawsuits filed by customers or employers.

d.   The political issues which affect organisations include those which influence the extent of government regulation. New legislation is introduced to take account of social pressure or new ways of operating. The privacy legislation introduced in 2001 has altered the way organisations can use and hold information on employees and customers.

4. The **socio-cultural element** is the element of the general environment that includes the attitudes, values, norms, beliefs, behaviours, and associated demographic trends that are characteristic of a given geographic area.

    a. The socio-cultural element is of particular importance to organisations as it tends to occur slowly but had a profound effect in how the organisation operates.

    b. Current changes in Australia: include the delay of marriage to a later age, the emergence of the single head of household, the aging of the large baby-boomer group, the growing shortage of workers ages 18 through 24, and the increasing influence of minorities.

    c. Socio-cultural trends can include attitudes for example the demand for quality, acceptance of internet transactions etc

5. The **international element** is the element of the general environment that includes the developments in countries outside an organisations home country that have the potential of impacting on the organisation.

    a. Fluctuations of the dollar against foreign currencies influence the ability of an organisation to compete in international markets, eg the currency problems in Asian countries in late 1997.

    b. New global competitors can gain a significant share of the domestic market.

    c. International unrest and conflict. The 'axis of evil' initiated by the USA, the fear of terrorism, the religious unrest and antagonism in trading nations such as Indonesia. The impact on Australia's airline travel and numbers of tourists and students arriving in Australia.

6. The **natural environment** is the element of the general environment that covers those aspects that effect an organisation by natural events such as drought, flood, pests etc. The inclusion of the environment is part of post modernism thinking. The impact can be direct for example the 2002 drought on farming particularly in northern NSW and Queensland. Or indirect for example Elders whose income comes from providing services to the rural community has been effected by the drought, the price of meat and certain vegetables has risen impacting on the food and restaurant industries.

Activity

Write down two issues that are impacting your organisation in each of the general environment areas.

International: _____

_____

Economic: _____

_____

Socio-cultural: _____

_____

Legal Political: _____

_____

Technical: _____

_____

Natural: _____

_____

Understanding of the General Environment

Your organisation is impacted by but cannot usually influence back the general environment elements. Usually an individual organisation is impacted by the elements in its general environment but is rarely able to put an influence back to change that element. For example most organisations may recognise the impact computers have on their organisation in enabling then to process data and to communicate. As an open system they may choose to accept the newest versions of programs/equipment or alternatively reject them. However they are usually unable to affect the direction or the type of technology being developed because they are individually too small to influence the state of knowledge.

- **System Thinking** Each of these elements is not independent. The change in one will affect other elements. For example the 2002 drought (Natural Event) affected the volume of grain exported and Australia's foreign exchange rate (international) the prosperity of the rural communities and the industries that service them declined and employment in this sector declined (economic). The relationship between the elements that will determine the impact on your organisation.

- **Select only those elements that are significant** The complexity of the system is enormous it is your specific as mangers to identify those elements that are dynamic and thus are important to recognise.

- **The general environment is common in most aspects for all operators in the specific industry.** Your general environment is similar to other organisation operating in the same industry. They will usually be experiencing the impact of similar trends

Specific Environment

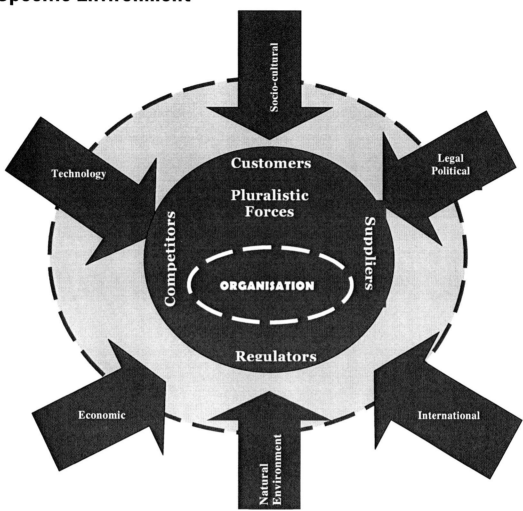

The **specific environment** is the segment of the external environment made up of the specific outside elements with which an organisation interfaces in the course of conducting its business.

The specific environment depends on the products and services the organisation offers and the locations where it conducts business.

1. An organisation's **customers and clients** are those individuals and organisations that purchase its products and/or services. They will dictate the quality, quantity variety of products and services product.

2. Organisations' **competitors** are other organisations that either offer or have a high potential of offering rival products or services.

    -   Organisations need to keep abreast of who their competitors are and what they are doing.

    -   Ways to track what competitors are doing include obtaining information from commercial data bases, specialty trade publications, news clippings from local newspapers, help-wanted ads, published market research reports, financial reports, trade shows, public filings, advertisements, and personal contacts.

3. An organisation's **suppliers** are those individuals and organisations that supply the resources (such as raw materials, products, or services) the organisation needs to conduct its operations. An organisation's **labour supply** consists of those individuals who are potentially employable by the organisation. It may also include sub-contractors or outsourced activities.

4. Various **regulation** you may have to abide and monitor compliance with laws and regulations at local (eg local council regulations, enterprise bargain agreements), state or regional (eg Awards, consumer affairs, trading hours legislation), and national (eg Equal Opportunity legislation) levels.

Activity

Diagnostic checklist for external environment analysis

It is often difficult to identify the relevant factors in the external marketplace environment which are likely to affect an individual organisation or unit. There are many external influences. They tend to be constantly changing in our turbulent environment, and may present potential opportunities at one point in time and potential threats at another.

The steps in external environment analysis are:

- Identify the relevant factors within the marketplace in which the organisation competes.

- Determine the sources of information (eg Australian Bureau of Statistics, reports on the economy, forecasts by professional firms, Financial press etc).

- Collect or obtain the information.

- Determine its relevance to the organisation as:

  – potential opportunities to be exploited; or

  – threats to be mitigated or avoided.

The following checklist presents a number of external environment factors headings that may be considered relevant. Due to the difficulties of defining and obtaining relevant information, assistance from a professional adviser may be warranted.

Check where relevant	Comment
1. Socio-cultural factors	
Population trends; ethnic group, growing suburbs household structure	
Characteristics of population: age, education	
Consumer values & tastes	
Changing attitudes of society	
Organised consumer groups and pressure groups	
2. Economic factors	
Projected interest rates, long term fixed rates	
Unemployment: location, age/skills, rate projected	

Industry sector trends: projected growth	
Productivity and labour costs trends	
Industry specific information: growth in demand projected, sales force information, industry inflation	
Demand factors: average disposable incomes, level of inflation, motor vehicle registrations, vacancy ratios in commercial and domestic properties	
Local economy: competitiveness	
International economics and trade (ie the 　　　- global marketplace) 　　　- competitiveness compared with 　　　- overseas companies 　　　- relative inflation rates	
3.　　Technology	
New technologies being developed, integration into industry	
New transport, production processes	
Changes affecting end use of products	
Risk of obsolesce, cost of adoption of new technologies	
Changes to packaging	
Relative changes within industry sectors	
4.　　Legal/political – Government	
Federal	
Industry assistance programs	
Tariffs and industry protection policies	
Trade practices	
Balance of payments	
Foreign trade policies	
Regulation of companies and securities	
Regulations regarding foreign companies	
Taxation	
Subsidies	
Recent court cases/precedents	
Environmental protection	
State	
Assistance programs	

Legislation	
Commercial regulations	
Taxes	
Environmental Protection	
Development restrictions	
Local government	
Development restrictions	
Environmental protection	
Rates and taxes	
Zoning bylaws	
5. The industry sector	
Growing or declining industry	
Cost of entry into and exit from the industry	

Industry restructuring:
    . improving competitiveness
    . benchmarking and best practice
    . acquisitions
    . mergers and rationalisations
    . vertical and horizontal integration	

Changes in sources of supply	
Total quality management	
Structural change	
Technical change	
Trade unions	
Specific industry assistance programs	
6. Customers and suppliers	
Their perceptions of the enterprise	
7. Competitors	

Competitors' strengths and weaknesses
    . finance and financial strength
    . Product range
    . Product quality
    . Marketing and channels of distribution
    . Market share
    . Price structure	

Adapted from: Flavel R, Williams J, Strategic Management: A Practical Approach, Prentice Hall, 1996	

The Macro Environment - A PEST Analysis

Source: Anderson & Woodcock, "Effective Entrepreneurship", Blackwell Publishers Ltd., USA 1996.

For our purpose here we are scanning the wider external environment primarily to seek opportunities. Of course, this macro analysis will also highlight problems and constraints emanating from this environment. One useful way to highlight this complex interaction of environmental influences is by a PEST - **political, economic, sociological and technological** - analysis, which will give us our checklist. It should act as an indicative *aide-memoir* and is not intended to be fully comprehensive.

Political

This list can be quite extensive and very complex. The political environment includes such factors as:

- The prevalent political ideology
- Power blocks and interest groups
- National or transnational sovereignties
- Government policies and regulations towards commerce/trade
- The legal framework including laws, codes or practice and regulations
- The degree of political stability conducive or otherwise towards business
- The degree of altruism in politics as opposed to pure greed and suchlike
- Nationalism
- Terrorism
- Quality standards
- Health, safety, and so on
- Government views/policies towards entrepreneurs and enterprise

The political dimension is very important, operating at various levels - international, national and local - and providing the context to the operation.

Political stability and ideology will add to the 'feel' of business, and laws will give a more formal context to enterprise. Political turbulence is the problem in some countries, while enterprise is strangled by red tape in other regions.

Economic

This part of the environment should be easier to understand and perhaps less volatile - depending upon the country. Some features include:

- The dominant economic system (eg pro/anti-nationalisation)
- Inflation/prices
- Poverty/income and wealth distribution/standards of living
- Global economic trends
- Taxation
- Economic aid for enterprise development
- Growth/decline at national level
- Types of market and so forth
- Trends in markets
- Customer type, preference and segments
- The availability of land, premises, equipment and capital
- Labour mix/availability
- Productive levels
- Fiscal policies impacting on enterprise

The economic scene can be 'managed' more than the political dimension as the information and intelligence ought to be more available to the entrepreneur.

Social/sociological

This part of the environment is very much concerned with the cultural and subculture of specific societies/subsocieties. To some extent it is linked to the economic aspects of the wider environment. Some issues may include:

- Value systems
- Tolerance/intolerance of entrepreneurs/enterprise
- Views towards risk taking
- The authority system (at work and in the wider society)
- Institutions
- Social mobility
- Gender and equality
- Race and equality
- Morality/ethics in general
- Views/beliefs in work and leisure
- Crime deviance and property

- Social mobility/immobility
- Religion and belief structures
- Social systems
- Class and social stratification
- The role of the family
- The work organisation
- Education and language
- Views of social responsibility in business

Social changes provide tremendous opportunities for the enterprising opportunists. These changes can signal new/markets, new segments, a need for new products/services of some change in the product/service.

Technical/technological

There seems to be nothing as consistent as change. Often this change is technologically driven. We are living through another industrial revolution at the moment and the impact on how we work and live is enormous.

Change always occurs, but of late, the pact of change has quickened. For example:

- The business can be extended by technical innovations
- Products/services can quickly become obsolescent
- Information and data is more readily available for everyone (including competitors)
- Design and development are key areas in most sectors
- Opportunities can come from the exploitation of innovation (eg new materials)
- Implications exist for capital, R & D and costs in general
- Implications exist for labour (eg from redundancy, short-time, deskilling to reskilling)
- Customers may need greater 'education'about new technology/changes in the technical sophistication of products/services

Relationships between the general environment, specific environment and an organisation's domain

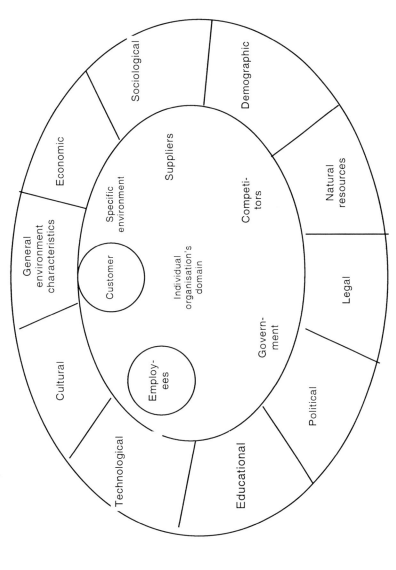

Source: adapted from F.E. Kast, 'Scanning the Future Environment: Social Indicators, California Management Review 23,1 (1980): 24.

UNIT 4

UNCERTAINTY

Understanding the Specific Environment

Each unit or organisation will face unique specific environment. No two organisations/units have the same specific environment, each unit or organisation will have unique customers, competitors, suppliers, labour etc

You are influenced by and your unit or organisation is able to influence the elements in its specific environment Your customers will effect how you operate through what the purchase, where and how. But in turn you can influence your customers decisions through such things as advertising, your choices to introduce a new product or service or to stop producing one etc. There is a two way process.

Pluralism

A pluralistic society is one in which many different groups and organisations have an effect on the operation of organisations and businesses. The literature supports the view that interest groups work in a range of ways to contribute to change in a society according to their particular interests.

England (1992) defines pluralism as "a society in which members of diverse ethnic, racial, religious and social groups maintain participation in, and development of their traditions and special interests, while cooperatively working toward the interdependence needed for a nation's unity". As a philosophy, this is supported in more political terms by Marcil-Lacoste (1992) whose definition includes the "self-regulation or self-administration of society through the competition of groups sharing the roles and privileges of the social domain".

"In a pluralist society, all institutions are of necessity political institutions. All are multi-constituency institutions ..." (Drucker, 1980), rather than the single-purpose institutions as which they started out. A single-purpose institution seeks to optimise outcomes (and is often in control of that optimisation). However, as suggested by Drucker, in a political process involving multiple parties, you do not try to optimise but to *satisfice*, that is to seek an 'acceptable compromise'. Drucker goes on to say that, as a pluralist society we need to demand that institutions take responsibility beyond their own specific mission. But in determining their range of responsibilities, managers need to be able to distinguish between what they can and cannot do. They should not take on responsibilities which impair the function of the primary task, but they also need to take into account the needs and impact of their constituencies.

Elements of a Pluralistic Society

Pluralism the fundamental framework within which business must live and grow
(rules of the game!)

Explanation

- Diverse groups maintain autonomous participation and influence in the social system.

- Business is influenced by these groups in its interface with them in the system (business exerts equal influence groups)

- Society challenges the business environment to refine and assert its core values while accommodating diversity.

Characteristics Historically Associated with Professional Groups

- Commitment to a distinct body of knowledge

- Specific and lengthy training

- Restrictive entry

- Prescribed code of ethics and standards of behaviour

- Proclaimed concern for client groups

- Peer group evaluation, control and promotion

Example

The Impact of Pluralism on Education

- The education environment too has had to reflect and respond to the composition of a wider population and are beginning to mirror the cultural pluralism of a wider society.

- Government policy now makes education (higher education) accessible to a wider cross section of the community

- This is apparent by the trend in escalating emphasis on marketing Australian education in neighbouring regions, resulting in an increasing presence of international students

- Education is now being treated as a commodity and is therefore marketed as such

Managers are responsible to a diverse set of stakeholders and have responsibilities to all of them[1]

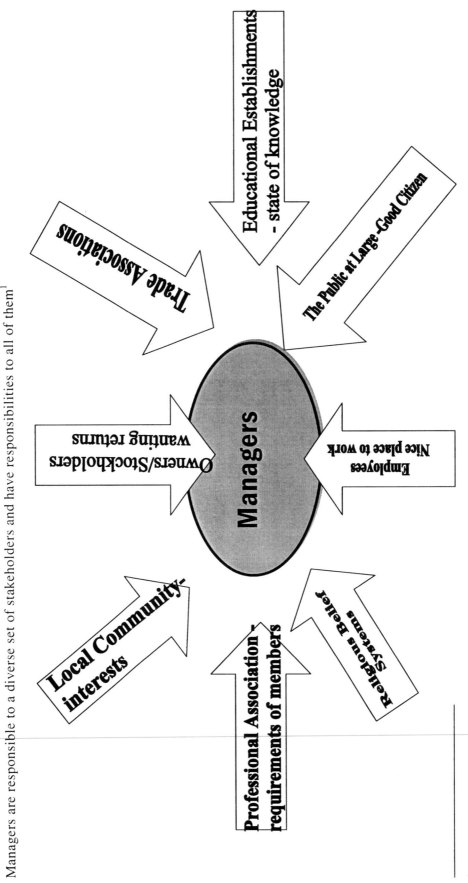

Using Your Knowledge of the Environment

Open system vs. Closed System The ability to recognise the impact of the general environment and specific on your industry and organisation and to react to these changes reflects the degree of openness of your system. A closed system is one that cannot recognise these trends and impacts.

Strategies Your organisation can recognise the impact of its general and specific environment by being open, but is it how it uses this information to develop strategies that is important.

Uncertainty effects organisation It is the uncertainty as to how the environment will impact that creates the problem

There are three perspectives used to describe how the environment affects organisations:

- Environmental change and complexity

- Environmental turbulence

- Levels of uncertainty

We will look at each of these before we discuss some mechanisms for analysing the environment and how competitive strategies are developed.

- Competitive forces

1. Assessing Environmental Uncertainty

Environmental uncertainty is a condition of the environment in which future conditions affecting an organisation cannot be accurately assessed and predicted.

- **Environmental complexity** refers to the number of elements in an organisations environment and their degree of similarity.

- **Environmental dynamism** refers to the rate and predictability of change in the elements of an organisations environment, ranging from slow and stable to fast and unstable.

- **Environmental uncertainty** can be assessed as a function of complexity and dynamism.

ENVIRONMENTAL DYNAMISM/COMPLEXITY

E	S	LOW UNCERTAINTY 1. Few, similar external elements 2. Elements stay the same or change slowly Cell 1	MODERATELY LOW UNCERTAINTY 1. Many dissimilar external elements 2. Elements stay the same or change slowly Cell 2
N	T		
V	A		
I	B		
R	L		
O	E		
N			
M	U	Cell 3 MODERATELY HIGH UNCERTAINTY 1. Few, similar external elements 2. Elements change rapidly and unpredictably	Cell 4 HIGH UNCERTAINTY 1. Many dissimilar external elements 2. Elements change rapidly and unpredictably
E	N		
N	S		
T	T		
A	A		
L	B		
	L		
	E		

          Homogenous   Heterogenous

ENVIRONMENTAL COMPLEXITY

Source: Adapted James Thompson 1968, Organisations in Action, McGraw-Hill.

This tells us about the sort of uncertainty an organisation faces but it does not indicate how to manage that uncertainty.

2. Turbulence

Ansoff Environmental Dependence Hypothesis -This hypothesis states that the challenges from the firm's environment determine the optimal mode of behaviour.

Managers need to consider three characters in their environment in order to assess its turbulence.

      a.   Familiarity of events (less familiar, greater the turbulence).

      b.   Rapidity of change (rapid change, greater the turbulence).

      c.   Visibility/predictability of the future / less predictable, greater the turbulence.

Concept of Strategic Flexibility

(The extent an organisation is able to respond to perceived environmental turbulence.)

Scale of environmental turbulence -Ansoff 1984

Inactive environment	Management strategy based on maintenance/preservation
Gentle Turbulence	Slow/obvious change - focus on doing best possible job/lowest feasible cost
Moderate Turbulence	External focus, aim identify/satisfy customer needs before competitors
Discontinuous Turbulence	Changes clear, but unable to predict when or how big. Focus - adaptability, so organisation can anticipate/react.
Unpredictable Turbulence (surprises)	focus - ongoing strategic analysis (rather than formal/periodic), experimentation creativity (ability to step back and look and avoid institutionalising successful behaviours of the past).

This concept gives a manager insight as it indicates that:

    –   No one approach is correct, different organisations/units may require different types of management practices

    –   Depending on the environment the organisation faces the managers should take a different approach.

Five Degrees of Change – John Kotter 2002

Different industries operate at different levels of change and thus need to use different approaches to succeed. Read through the five degrees of change listed below, then continue on to see how the degrees of change relate to different types of leadership and winning in the new economy.

1	**Little change** Making goods and services with long product life cycles.
2	**Continuous improvement** Constant incremental changes in products and ways of operating.
3	**Non-incremental change within businesses** In addition to degree 2, regularly introducing new product lines and significant improvements in how to run the business.
4	**Whole new businesses** In addition to degrees 2 and 3, inventing not just new product lines but new businesses.
5	**Whole new business models** In addition to degrees 2, 3, and 4, inventing not just new businesses but new economic and organizational models.

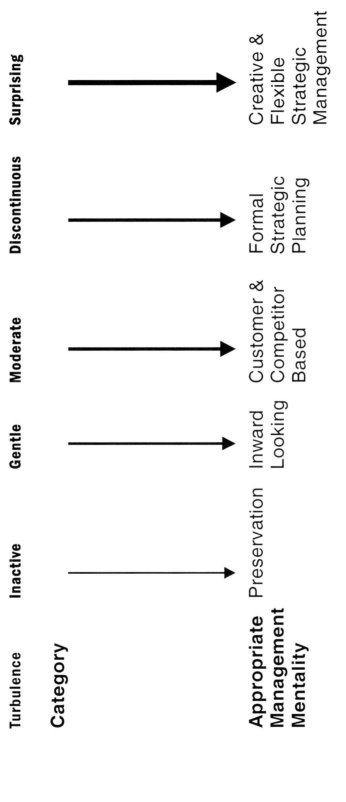

Turbulence Category	Inactive	Gentle	Moderate	Discontinuous	Surprising
Appropriate Management Mentality	Preservation	Inward Looking	Customer & Competitor Based	Formal Strategic Planning	Creative & Flexible Strategic Management

Matching Turbulence – Aggressiveness - Responsiveness[2]

ENVIRONMENTAL TURBULENCE	REPETITIVE repetitive	EXPANDING Slow, incremental	CHANGING Fast, incremental	DISCONTINUOUS Discontinuous, predictable	SURPRISEFUL Discontinuous, unpredictable
STRATEGIC AGGRESSIVENESS	STABLE Stable based on precedents	REACTIVE Incremental` based con experience	ANTICIPATORY Incremental based on extrapolation	ENTREPRENEURIAL Discontinuous. New based on observable opportunities	CREATIVE Discontinuous. Novel based on creativity
ORGANISATIONAL RESPONSIVENESS	STABILITY SEEKING Rejects change	EFFICIENCY DRIVEN Adapts to change	MARKET DRIVEN Seeks familiar change	ENVIRONMENT-ALLY DRIVEN Seeks related change	ENVIRONMENT CREATING Seeks novel change
RESPONSIVENESS OF CAPABILITY	CUSTODIAL Precedent driven	PRODUCTION Efficiency driven	MARKETING Market driven	STRATEGIC Driven by the environment	FLEXIBLE Seeks to create the environment
	Suppresses change	Adapts to change	Seeks familiar change	Seeks new change	Seeks novel change
	Seeks stability		Seeks operating efficiency		Seeks creativity
	Closed system				Open system
TURBULENCE LEVEL	LOW				HIGH

[2] Adapted from Ansoff,I. (1990) 'General Management in Turbulent Environments', *Practising Manager*, Vol 11, No 1, pp 6-27 in Hubard, G. (2000) Strategic Management: Thinking, Analysis and Action, Pearson Education, Frenchs Forest p 43.

3. Level of uncertainty

The uncertainty facing a decision can vary. Adapting an article in the Harvard Business Review, Nov-Dec 1997 by Hugh Courtney, Jane Kirkland and Patrick Viguerie on 'Strategies under Uncertainty', for general decision-making we can categories uncertainty into four levels.

a. Clear-enough future

Managers can develop a single forecast of the future that is precise enough for decision making. The future uncertainty is sufficiently known to allow a decision.

Examples may be predicting the sales level and costs of a product for the year ahead or the impact of purchasing a piece of capital equipment.

Forecasting techniques or tools managers use to assist predicting the future are such things as break-even analysis, cost-benefit analysis etc and in the longer term they use such things as Net Present Values. These methods are discussed in such courses as Managing Finance-Operating & Capital Expenditure and Managing Group Problem Solving & Decision Making.

b. Alternative futures

The future can be described as one of a few alternative outcomes or discrete scenarios. Managers cannot identify which outcome will occur, although it may help establish probabilities.

Examples would be Telstra assessing the impact of privatisation of its market, new product distribution alternatives.

Change may occur in major steps at some particular point in time (eg due to legislative change) or the change may be more gradual in an evolutionary fashion (eg technological standards, quality standards, environmental). Forecasting techniques used would be based not only in identifying the different possible future outcomes but also to think through the alternative ways of reaching the alternative future.

c. Range of futures

A range of potential futures can be identified. The range is defined by a limited number of key variables, but the actual outcome may lie anywhere along a continuum bounded by that range. There are no discrete scenarios.

Examples include the entering of new or emerging markets, developing or acquiring emerging technologies.

The forecasting methods appropriate to this level of uncertainty would be technology forecasting, scenario planning and latent-demand research.

d.   True ambiguity

Uncertainty in the environment is virtually impossible to predict. No range of outcomes is possible to predict. This level of ambiguity is rare as managers seek to break down the uncertainty into shorter timeframes, or smaller decision levels.

The forecasting methods tend to be more qualitative. Managers seek to catalogue systematically what they know and what is possible to know.

Examples: In 1990 impact of Internet on business and personal lives.

This model is useful because it tells us that:

- The level of uncertainty dictates the forecasting method used. The last three levels of uncertainty, alternative futures, range of futures and true ambiguity are those areas that crete the greatest uncertainty.

- The methods of evaluating choices under 'a clear enough future' are easy you can assume you will continue doing things as you have historically

- The level of uncertainty raises also with the horizon, the longer the horizon the more variables there are and the more difficult it is to forecast.

HOW TO USE THE FOUR LEVELS OF UNCERTAINTY

	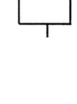	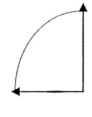	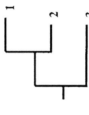	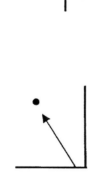
What Can Be Known?	• A single forecast precise enough for determining strategy	• A few discrete outcomes that define the future	• A range of possible outcomes, but no natural scenarios	• No basis to forecast the future
Analytic Tools	• "Traditional" strategy tool kit	• Decision analysis • Option valuation models • Game theory	• Latent-demand research • Technology forecasting • Scenario planning	• Analogies and pattern recognition • Nonlinear dynamic models
Examples	• Strategy against low-cost airline entrant	• Long-distance telephone carriers' strategy to enter deregulated local-service market • Capacity strategies for chemical plants	• Entering emerging markets, such as India • Developing or acquiring emerging technologies in consumer electronics	• Entering the market for consumer multi-media applications • Entering the Russian market in 1992

Source: Courtney, Kirkland, Viguerie, Harvard Business Review, Nov-Dec 1997, p67-79

UNIT 5

FORECASTING: QUALITATIVE METHODS

There are different ways of assessing your general and specific environment. With high levels of uncertainty organisations are utilising more advances methods of predicting the future.

Forecasting:

1. Scenarios as a method for understanding uncertainty

2. Qualitative

3. Quantitative

Paradigms

Paradigms are defined as a set of rules and regulations (written or unwritten) that do two things:

1. Some of the rules establish the edges or boundaries of a territory.

2. The rest of the rules tell us how to act within those boundaries to achieve some measure of success. For example, when we say "let me show you how we do things around here", we are giving rules that tell us how to act.

Source: Joel Barjer, Paradigms Video.

A paradigm is a preconceived idea of what the world is, what it should be like, and how it should operate. These ideas or beliefs become so deeply embedded in our minds that they are barriers to creative thinking, even though they may be outdated, obsolete and no longer relevant. They act as barriers to your ability to be unbiased in your expectations of the future because they make you make assumptions about the future based often on the continuation of the past.

In short, paradigms act as a barrier to seeing the reality. For example, read the following aloud:

PARIS	ONCE	BIRD
IN THE	IN A	IN THE
THE SPRING TIME	A LIFE TIME	THE HAND

Source: p53, Entrepreneurship and New Venture Formation, Zimmer Thomas & Scarborough Norman, Prentice Hall, 1996.

Most people do not notice the extra word in each phrase. Why? Because we don't see it! Past experience shapes the way we perceive the world around us.

Quality of the forecast

Data, raw facts such as the number of customers, may not help managers make decisions.

Managers need information; data arranged in a meaningful fashion. Good information processes the characteristics.

- Quality: measures information, accuracy and reliability
- Timeliness: information is needed when managerial action is taken
- Completeness: manager has information to act
- Relevance: information matches the manager's specific needs.

Therefore, quality of a forecast depends on the following questions:

- How well it meets the decision needs. Does the forecast meet the purpose or objective of the decision maker? Will the information you gain help you make a decision?
- Is there sufficient lead time to undertake appropriate forecasting methods? Time constraints may mean that you have to use less effective forecasting techniques. Will these provide for reliable decision-making?
- How well are forecasting methodologies applied? How good is the data?
- Can the forecast be revised or updated?
- Will cost constraints reduce the range of forecasting methods available? Will this require you to produce a less reliable forecast?
- Do the decision makers understand the limitations of forecasting techniques and the assumptions made?

Eight barriers to understanding

Decision makers are frequently surprised by events. They tend to extrapolate present trends into the future without giving any consideration to other "wild card" alternatives. Fred Kierstead and Christopher Dede identified eight reasons for this:

1. Reliance on technological solutions

2. Cultural blindness (ethnocentricity)

3. Narrow data bases

4. Failure to recognise normative issues (i.e. set paradigms)

5. Concentrate on one probable future

6. Ignorance of the world outside the company (internalisation)

7. Locked into a time period (tempocentrism, concentrating on current trends as continuing)

8. Failure to communicate.

Adapted from: Eight Barriers to Understanding, Chapter 6, Kierstead F, Dede C, 'Understanding Business Forecasting', Graceway Publishing, 1988.

The scenario method

As outlined in the previous unit different levels of uncertainty require different types of forecasting. In this session we will initially at scenario planning which is used when there are high levels of uncertainty due to such things as rapidly changing technology, a highly turbulent market, etc. The next section looks at using other forecasting methods, qualitative when you are unable to use the past as an indicator of the future and in the next unit quantitative methods when you can use the past as a good indication of the future.

Since standard forecasting methods cannot "reveal" the future, the prospective approach has shifted in recent years towards presentation of small numbers of scenario hypotheses, each constructed as a coherent representation of possible futures. Clearly, there is no single applicable scenarios approach; nonetheless, we have decided to present the most commonly used method.

What is a scenario?

> *Scenario: "a description of a future situation and the course of events which allows one to move forward from the original situation to the future situation".*

Two major categories of scenario can be identified:

- **exploratory:** starting from past and present trends and leading to a likely future;

- **anticipatory or regulatory:** build on the basis of different visions of the future; they may be either desired or, on the contrary, feared.

These anticipatory or exploratory scenarios may, moreover, be trend-driven or contrasted, depending on whether they incorporate the most likely or the most unlikely changes.

Phase 1: Building the base

This phase plays a fundamental role in scenario construction. It requires representation of the present state of the system (the enterprise or its environment). Thus, one must:

1. identify the system and its environment and identify the main variables

2. analyse the environment.

Once the key factors and analysis have been conducted, we can list the possible futures via a set of hypotheses, which point to continuation of a trend or, on the other hand, its cessation. As these hypotheses are implemented, we are then faced with an identifiable degree of uncertainty that the expert method can endeavour to clarify.

Phase 2: Scanning the range of future possibilities and reducing uncertainty

Phase 3: Building the scenarios

At this point, the scenarios are still embryonic since they are restricted to sets of hypotheses, whether implemented or not. The next stage is to describe the pathways that lead from the current situation to the final situation for the scenario.

Phase 4: Evaluating and choosing possible strategic policies

Scenarios throw indispensable light on the process of orienting strategic decisions. The scenarios method can help in deciding on the most appropriate strategy to be deployed, with the maximum of assets, in order to attain the targeted aims.

However, although the sequence is logical, it need not necessarily be followed rigidly from start to finish; much depends on one's degree of familiarity with the system under study and the aims. The scenario method is modular and one can, where necessary, limit the study to a given set of modules, eg:

- structural analysis and the search for the key variables
- analysis of actors' strategies
- questioning of experts about future hypotheses.

One of the main constraints of the scenarios method is time. It generally takes from 12 to 18 months to follow the path through completely and half of this time is taken up just building the base. If one only has 3 to 6 months to finalise the study, it is preferable to concentrate efforts on whatever is considered to be the most important module. Of the case studies given above, a fully implemented scenario method was used in less than half of the examples.

Prospects are clear: the scenario method will continue to play a reference role, but will only occasionally be used in its entirety. Such use will be restricted to specialists involved in particularly long pieces of work.

References (scenarios)

Look up the internet under "forecasting" and "scenarios".

Key messages from scenario planning

- Business revisioning is the most risky form of corporate re-engineering.
- The risks are mainly functional and political.
- Scenario analysis is a method of anticipating the future without bias.
- Scenario analysis reduces the risk of revisioning by establishing consent about the future and ensures that neither too little nor too much is attempted currently.
- Scenario analysis establishes a range of future scenarios. Those deemed critical are known as "the driving uncertainties".
- These driving uncertainties establish a new corporate vocabulary for a discussion on business change. The discussion process is internally owned.
- The range of scenarios allows current actions to be judged more accurately against all possible features.
- The technique is therefore an essential element for the safe management of corporate change.

Developing Scenarios

1. Define the scope

    *   Time Frame

2. Identify the Major Stakeholders

    *   Who will have an interest in these issues

    *   Who will be affected by them?

    *   Who could influence them?

3. Identify Basic Trends

4. Identify Key Uncertainties

    *   What events, whose outcomes are uncertain, will significantly affect the issues you are concerned with?

5. Construct Initial Scenario Theme

6. Check for Consistency and Plausibility

7. Develop Learning Scenarios

8. Identify Research Needs

9. Develop Quantitative Models

10. Evolve Towards Decision Scenarios

Activity

1. Given the prediction of the aging population of Australia in 2051, what impact is this going to have in terms of:

    *   Social

    *   Economic

    *   Politics

    *   Science and Technology?

2. What do you predict will happen in the following industries?

    *   Airlines

    *   Apparel

    *   Cosmetics

    *   Consumer electronics

    *   Home furnishings

    *   Leisure time

- Restaurants
- Retailing

3. Can you categorise the uncertainty facing these industries in terms of:

- Clear enough future
- Alternative futures
- A range of futures, or
- True ambiguity?

Statistical profile

The projections show that the ageing of Australia's population will continue. This is the inevitable result of fertility remaining at low levels over a long period associated with increasing life expectancy. As growth slows, the population ages progressively with the median age of 35 years in 1999 increasing to 40–42 years in 2021 and 44-47 years in 2051.

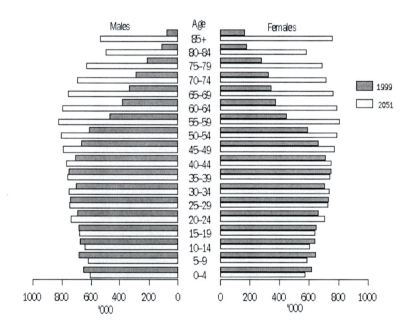

2051 PROJECTED POPULATION AGE STRUCTURE, Series II - Australia

By 2051, the population aged 65 years and over is projected to be at least double its present size, increasing from 12% of the population in 1999 to 24-27% in 2051. In Series II, the highest annual rate of growth for this age group will occur in 2012 when the large cohort born in 1947, part of the post World War II 'baby boom', turns 65.

The 85 years and over age group numbered 241,100 (1.3% of the total population) in 1999. This group is projected to reach approximately 1.3 million in 2051, and between 1.3 million and 1.6 million in 2101.

In 1999, the 85 years and over age group was dominated by women, who made up 69% of the group. In all series this proportion is projected to fall to 63% in 2021, 59% in 2051 and 57% in 2101, reflecting the increase in life expectancy of men and the narrowing gap in life expectancy between men and women.

The population aged 15-64 years, which encompasses much of the working-age population, made up 67% of Australia's population in 1999. This proportion increases slightly over the first ten years of the projection under all the main series to reach 68% in 2008. It then declines to 65% in 2021, 59-60% in 2051 and 58-59% in 2101.

Source: Australian Bureau Of Statistic Web site Jan 2002
'Population Projections'.

Activity

Scenario setting

> Any astronomer can predict just where every star will be at half past eleven tonight: he can make no such prediction about this daughter.
>
> *James Truslow Adams*

Consider this statement about a day in the future

Time: August 10, 2020, Friday, 7:00   *Place*: Royal Adelaide Hospital

Nursing staff have been on duty for an hour. They have attended the handover from the Nursing Coordinator and they are now moving towards their cars ready to visit their patients. Their cars are fully equipped with a portable monitoring system, which includes a number of testing kits, VDU, computer and electronic scanning equipment. This allows the nurse to perform X-rays, scans, blood and other tests; it also allows the sending of reports to the medical officer allocated at the hospital. The scanner also records vital signs and, by the flick of a switch. Documents all the findings on an electronic medical record. The nursing staff case manages a group of patients based on their medical condition and their suburb. The patients are visited at their home, appropriate information is transmitted to the medical officer, who can interpret the data and prescribe ongoing treatment.

The cost reduction and success of the program has resulted in 80% of all patients being treated in this way. The Royal Adelaide Hospital now consists principally as a Day Surgery and Casualty Service with only five wards remaining to cater for intensive care patients and accident victims.

This little scenario or view about the future contains a number of predictions or forecasts.[1] These predictions are all time specific, in that a definite time and date are specified, together with a particular location.

There is absolutely no possibility of the scenario being fully accurate about what will occur. At this point one cannot forecast the future perfectly, that is without error. It does not require much imagination to realise how dull and mentally debilitating life would be if everything about the future were known with complete accuracy. Fortunately, such a possibility is by no means in sight.

Let us examine some of the details of the scenario.

1. *The date*

    • August 10, 2020 merely specifies when the scenario is to occur.

2. *The day*

    • That this date will be a Friday is not a forecast but merely a designation of a name to a date according to a widely accepted method of designating names, known as the Gregorian calendar. This calendar has given such names to all dates into the indefinite future. An assumption is being made that the same calendar will be in use in 2020.

3. *Event*

    • With the introduction of microsurgery and the enormous predictions for genetics, it is expected that much of the hospitalisation of individuals will be obsolete. Organ replacement will remove the need to treat such diseases as heart disease, diabetes, liver failure, kidney failure etc. New organs or simply an injection of the appropriate cells will mean that these long-term diseases will disappear

4. *Cost Pressures*

    • There will be ongoing pressure to reduce the cost of medical treatment. These will continue. Hospitals are extremely expensive to run, and are often located on prime real estate. This is likely to continue. Research could be also conducted into the other pressures to reduce hospital sizes such as infection rates and growing risk of contracting infection.

5. *Personal behaviour*

    • Much of this is very doubtful, requiring not only that there are nurses around in 2020 and that they will treat people this way

---

[1] The words prediction and forecast will be considered to be completely interchangeable in what follows.

Even this simple scenario brings out a number of important points about forecasting. The most important of these is that things to be forecasted vary greatly in their degree of predictability. Whereas some variables can be predicted with considerable accuracy, others are almost entirely unpredictable, as will be shown later. It should also be clear that the methods that can be used to forecast can vary greatly and will depend upon data availability, the quality of models available, and the kinds of assumptions made, amongst other things. This means that forecasting is generally not easy, which is one reason why the topic is so interesting.

Activity

Create a scenario of some event in 2010.

Provide supporting evidence that substantiates your predictions. For example, what parts of your scenario are unpredictable and why?

Forecasting research

The first part of the forecasting for your unit's future requires you to determine a future decision. Will I close down outlet X, should I redesign the product to meet a new market group etc. **The decision comes first**, only once you have an understanding of the decision can you then consider the quantities or events that require prediction.

What quantities or events require prediction?

The forecast prediction almost always becomes clear once the decision has been clarified. For example, if you are having to make a decision as to whether to launch a new type of gym shoe then the quantity or event requiring prediction will include the demand for gym shoes in the future. If the decision is whether to sign a 10-year agreement with a supplier at a guaranteed price then you would need to predict likely supply and demand trends, possible impact of new technology etc.

What quantities of events require prediction?

"Commercial forecasting is not a matter of sitting alone in your office while collecting and analysing facts. Rather like all organisational activities, it is a group exercise requiring the establishment of an organisational system."

"The effectiveness of a forecast is determined by how well it drives the decision system."

"A good forecast will convince others that, say, some assumption built into the company's plan is a myth."

(p2 Metcalfe, Mike)

Explorative research

What information and resources are available and how employable are they in your forecast, requires some explorative research prior to working out the forecasting process.

Explorative information collection is used when you are seeking an insight into the general nature of the problem, the decision alternatives relevant variables that need to be considered and the availability of existing experts, research or forecasts.

Typically this is what you would do to provide a context to the decision so that you can make informed forecasting decisions. The previous exercise requiring you to access key words on the Internet or CD ROM would be typical of this explorative research. However, you would go further by referencing relevant articles/books, university papers etc, checking company procedures and systems for collecting information, company records so that you had a good idea of what information is available and where and how you could potentially use it. This is not usually a lengthy or costly process.

Data/Information sources

Information/Data sources can be classified as either Secondary or Primary.

Secondary sources are already published data collected for purposes other than the specific forecasting or research needs.

Primary sources involve all the methods of original data collection. This type of data is often collected using sampling procedures, panel surveys, or a complete census of the item of interest or it may involve recording company statistics.

1.   Secondary sources

External sources

In recent years there has been a tremendous increase in the quantity of published data available to managers. The realisation of business and government managers that more and better information increases the effectiveness of planning and decision-making has contributed to this.

The government of Australia is the largest publisher and collector of data, general information is available through the Australian Bureau of Statistics through the census or industry statistics, while separate departments collect information on their specific areas.

Other sources of information and data include:

- The Australian Public Affairs Information Services (APAIS)
- Journals and magazines, eg Business Review Weekly, Retail World
- University and private research organisations
- Professional associations, eg Motor Traders Association, Australian Society of CPAs etc and their industry magazines and reports

- Books
- Internet (though the source of information needs to be verified).

Private/Internal sources

In addition to data collected from external sources, managers and forecasters can collect information from within their organisation. Computer systems have allowed a variety of information to be collected and stored so that they can be available when needed. Management 'information systems is a set of people, data, technology and organisational procedures that work together to retrieve, process, store and disseminate information to support decision making and control'

Dessler, Gary, Management, Prentice Hall, 1998, p617.

Information systems are more than computers. Managers at each level of the organisation have unique information requirements. Various types of information systems have thus been developed to serve the needs at each management level.

These systems have boosted the depth and range of information available. Examples of the sort of information available are product sales, staff turnover, production costing, R & D expenditure etc.

2. Primary sources

Survey data

Surveying customers, the general public, suppliers, experts and employees are a major source of primary data. The purpose of the data collection effort is to find out what the selected person thinks about key issues. The data collected might be a once-off effort or it may be repeated periodically.

When forecasters require an extensive amount of data from a large number of people they may use a survey, usually conducted via mail, personal interviews or by telephone.

There is a high degree of skill required to develop the survey and to determine how to select the sample.

Sampling

Frequently you can collect information from counting observations. For example, you can go through the visa/bankcard dockets and record the suburbs of purchasers or you can record the number of people entering a shop etc.

Test markets

The forecaster arranges for the placement of a new product into a 'typical' market area, and then observes the reaction to the product over a period of time.

3. Expert sources

There is usually a number of 'experts' who can provide background knowledge and information on the future. This expertise may come from: consultant researchers, industry experts, accountants, bankers, chambers of manufacture, government departments, retired industry players, academics, community organisations.

Activity

Shoes survey

Good morning/afternoon/evening. My name is………………………………and I am conducting a short survey on use of exercise shoes. Do you have a few moments to answer a few questions?

Date:_____ Time: _____

Gym: _____ M / F

1. What shoes do you currently use when attending this Gym?

2. Would you be interested in purchasing disposable Gym shoes?

3. What benefits would these have if they where mage available at this centre?

   - More hygienic

   - Less weight to carry

   - Other_____

4. How often do you attend this gym.

5. Have you come here from:

Work (go to 4)?	1
Home?	2
Other (specify)	3

6. If from work, in what suburb? _____

5. How regularly do you shop at Westpoint?

More than once a week	1
Once a week	2
Fortnightly	3
Once a month	4
Other (specify)	5

This is the first page of a survey conducted by marketing students for a project in their course. Can you identify the types of questions they have used? What difficulties do you think they might have had while conducting the survey in the shopping centre?

Some of the more commonly used question types are as follows.

Closed-end questions

Dichotomous questions – these offer just two answer choices

Multiple-choice questions – these offer three or more answers choices

Scaling questions – these invite respondents to indicate, for example, the extent of agreement with a statement, the level of importance to themselves of a particular attribute, or simply their rating, from 'poor' to 'excellent', of a particular variable.

Open-end questions

Unstructured questions – these allow respondents to offer their opinions on or attitudes to a variable completely in their own words.

Word associations – here respondents are asked to say the first word that comes to mind when shown a particular work (relating to the study).

Sentence or story completions – here respondents are invited to continue an incomplete sentence or story.

Validity/reliability of data collection methods

For data to be valid and reliable then you need to ensure that you can answer the following questions. This is particularly relevant to the secondary data.

- **Who?** This relates to the reputation of the collecting agency (do they have a reputation for quality research, do they have good information systems from which data is gathered). Also relevant is whether there is a sponsoring organisation or a bias or pressure group who would impact on the objectivity of the data collection. This is particularly important for information collected from the Internet, it is critical that you check the credentials of the source and consider any bias or selectiveness in data or information presented. A related question is whether the organisation has the necessary know-how or resources to develop the data. For example, an Internet site for a large company may look similar to that of a one-person show.

- **How?** It is impossible to appraise the quality of data without a knowledge of the methodology used to collect it. You should be suspicious of any secondary data source that does not include a description of the collection process, e.g. sample size, copy of questionnaire (if any), response rate, the source population etc. For primary data you should be able to describe how the data was collected.

- **Why?** Data that is collected to further the interest of a particular group are especially suspect. A tobacco company is not likely to release information that demonstrates the dangers of smoking.

- **What?** Even if the available data are of acceptable quality, they may prove difficult to use because they include non-relevant data, the data may be categorised differently or the area covered may be wrong. For example, use of Standard Industry Classification System to obtain information from the Bureau of Statistics, tends to group a large number of items into each classification by the state or for the whole of Australia. This makes it difficult to get relevant data on one item, e.g. gym shoes out of all footwear data.

- **Consistency?** Are there several sources of data that show consistent results? Conflicting results make the decision making difficult.

Interpretation of forecasts

One of the first things any student of forecasts must learn is that figures can be interpreted wrongly very easily. Hence, sayings such as "you can prove anything with figures" and "there are lies, damn lies and statistics". Because of their experience many people distrust forecasts. It is necessary to learn to look critically at all conclusions derived from forecasts.

1. **Biased sources** – All too often public statements that rely on statistics are unfortunately biased. To test such a statement you need to ask yourself, "who says this?", "why does he say it?" and "how does he know"? It should be appreciated though, that to say a source is biased does not mean that the statement is a deliberate lie but only that the person concerned has understandably picked the figures which will show his caste in the best light.

Examples:

(1) "75 percent of the voters voted for me. Most people in this constituency, then, must want me as their MP." What if less than two-thirds of the people voted – or half were not even on the electoral roll?

(2) "We interviewed 500 employees in the works canteen. 95 percent used our product, so it must be good." What if it was your own canteen and you operated a special discount scheme for your employees? Or even that you had a monopoly of the product (e.g. you were an Electricity Board)?

(3) "Nine out of ten female TV stars genuinely believe our product is the best." Did the tenth change her mind after she had been selected?

(4) "Nobody has ever put forward a justifiable complaint as to the way we handle matters." Who decides what is justifiable?

(5) "All the best looking people in this town buy our soap." How do you know they do? How do you know they are the best looking? What do they do with the soap – send it as a gift?

(6) "Since Mr Jones became Chief Constable arrests have gone up 50 percent." Maybe, but what about convictions?

(7) "Analysis of records shows that 75 percent of our students double their pay within ten years of taking our course." Analysis of other records may show that age, inflation and initiative result in 80 percent of all students doubling their pay within ten years of taking any course.

2.   **Invalid arguments** – A source may have no bias at all yet it is still very easy for a speaker to put forward an invalid argument. To test this one should ask oneself, "Does this follow"?

(1) "Party X has doubled its votes since the last parliamentary election. This proves that its support is greater than ever." If, in fact, three times as many candidates stood for election then the argument is invalid. Very probably the support has always been there – but it was not until the "last election" that it had the opportunity of showing itself in the form of votes.

(2) "No candidate for whom Harry has voted has even won an election. Therefore, Harry can stop a candidate winning by voting for him." Harry is the sort of person who votes for causes which are already lost – he does not make them losing causes by voting for them.

(3) "You're safe driving with me. I've never had an accident." Just passed your test? Besides, many accidents occur as a result of what someone else does.

(4) "More people die in bed than anywhere else. Bed, then, is the most dangerous place in the world!"

(5) "Tea kills!" Questioning persons involved in serious accidents disclosed that 95 percent had drunk tea with the previous 12 hours.

(6) "Not one out of 3,000 people interviewed at random had ever seen a polar bear roaming freely in England. Polar bears, then, don't roam freely in England." There's a high probability that the same 3,000 people would say they had never seen the Mayor of Middlewich but that would hardly prove he did not exist. Moreover, those 3,000 people could all be natives of Peru. Note here that although the argument is invalid, the conclusion is still correct. Do not, then, confuse an invalid conclusion with a false one.

(7) "The dollar went up by 50 percent last year. This year it has dropped by only 40 percent. So the dollar is worth more now than it was at the beginning of last year." If the dollar was worth, say, 100 at the beginning of last year it ended the year at 150. If it then dropped 40 percent it dropped to $150 - 40$ percent of $150 = 90$. So it's now worth less than at the start.

3.   **Alternative explanations** – Sometimes a fallacy in an argument is easier to detect if you ask yourself, "is there any other possible explanation?" Any statistical conclusion depends upon certain assumptions. These assumptions may or may not be warranted. Thus, the argument at the beginning of the section regarding the chance of Mr Smith's admission to Smithville hospital assumed that he belonged to the same class of people *as regards sex* as those who entered the hospital. In fact, he belonged to the same class only as regards place of residence.

(1) "Hospital records show that the number of people being treated for this disease has doubled in the last 20 years. Twice as many people, therefore, suffer from this disease that did 20 years ago." Possibly more people go to hospital today when they have this disease or, possibly, 20 years ago diagnosis was less accurate and they were treated for something else.

(2) "Theatres are fuller in London than in Paris. What nonsense to say that the English are less theatre-conscious than the French." There could be fewer theatres in London, or possibly the theatres outside London are considerably emptier than those outside Paris.

(3) "More professional people buy X paper than any other paper. This shows X's ideas and policies are in tune with modern professional thoughts." On the other hand, it could be that X carries the best "Situations Vacant" column.

(4) "More and more families travel today by car. This proves our standard of living is going up in leaps and bounds." Or could it be railway fares?

(5) "Last year 700 employees produced 150,000 ladders. This year 650 employees produced 160,000 ladders. This shows we have increased our productivity." Or decreased ladder sizes.

(6) "Mortgage conditions are causing large numbers of people to be homeless. Only 50 percent of the mortgage applications received last year were accepted by building societies." Possibly applicants applied twice.

(7) "Bosses' pay went up by 5 percent last year, while workers' pay went up 10 percent. The pay gap is narrowing." If the bosses' pay rose from $100,000 a year to $105,000 while the workers' pay rose from $5,000 to $5,500 the gap has grown by $4,500.

Hints for data gathering

1   Government or international organisations' statistics need to be examined carefully before use. Country and product definitions can differ considerably between the data agencies.

2   Many statistics are unreliable because of collection methods and definitional problems. There is often little that can be done about this situation.

3   Indices are often revised heavily and rebating can cause apparent step changes. Extreme caution is needed when carrying out regression analyses using recent data of this sort.

4   Industry statistics produced by industry federations are usually much more reliable than government statistics and should be used wherever possible.

5   As a result of the prevalence of 'dirty data':

   i.   Use good quality data wherever possible – the quality range is large.

ii. Use data which are counted rather than estimated wherever possible. For example, use demographic statistics in preference to production indices in a regression equation.

iii. The prevalence of 'dirty data' will inflate theoretical confidence limits considerably. Be realistic in this area.

iv. Weight recent data more heavily than data from long ago which may have definitional incompatibilities. But beware of index number revisions.

v. Do not dodge the pain of collecting high-quality data. Do not underestimate the time and expert knowledge needed to do this.

Chain-step Method

This method is based on the notion that it may be easier to estimate the separate components which then added together give a better example of the actual information you whant.

Example A brewery is interested in estimating the market potential for a new diabetic beer.

A forecast can be made by creating a chain as follows:

Demand for the new diabetic beer =

Population	x
personal discretionary income per capita	x
average percentage of amount spent on food that is spent on beverages	x
average percentage of amount that is spent on alcoholic beverages	x
average percentage of amount spent on alcoholic beverages that is spent on beer	x
expected percentage of amount spent on beer that will be spent on diabetic beer	x

So if you can get the figures for each of these or their trends then you can come up with a prediction of what diabetic beer consumption will be likely. If the population is 20,000,000, discretionary income per person averages out to be $10,000 then $200,000,000,000 is the amount available to spend on beverages. If 10% is the percentage of amount spent on food that is spent on beverages etc.

Appropriate forecast methods

Below is a list of possible forecasting methods. We will touch on all of these methods, the choice of which is appropriate will depend on what information/data you can gather, the level of uncertainty and the time horizon.

A Guide to Selecting an Appropriate Forecasting Method

Forecasting Method	Data Pattern	Quantity of Historical data (Number of Observations)	Forecast Horizon	Quantitative Background
Qualitative Methods				
– Role Playing	ANY	Little	Short to medium	Little
– Customer Surveys	Not applicable	None	Medium to long	Knowledge of survey methods
– Jury of executive opinion	ANY	None	ANY	Little
– Delphi	ANY	None	Long	Little
Quantative Methods				
Naïve	Stationary	1 or 2	Very Short	None
Moving Averages	Stationary	Number equal to the periods in the moving average	Very Short	Very Little
Exponential Smoothing				
– Simple	Stationary	5 to 10	Short	Little
– Adaptive Response	Stationary	10 to 15	Short	Moderate
– Holt's	Linear Trend	10 to 15	Short to medium	Little
– Winter's	Trend and seasonality	At least 4 or 5 per	Short to medium	Moderate
Regression-based				
– Trend	Linear and non-linear	Minimum of 10 with 4 or 5 per season if seasonality is included	Short to medium	Little

– Casual	Can handle nearly all patterns	Minimum of 10 per independent variable	Short, medium and long	Moderate
Time-series decomposition	Can handle trend, seasonal and cyclical patterns	Enough to see 2 peaks and troughs in the cycle	Short, medium and long	Little
ARIMA	Stationary or transformed to stationary	Minimum of 50	Short, medium and long	High

Forecasts can be categorised into two groups:

- quantitative
- qualitative.

Qualitative methods do not involve manipulation of data; only the judgement of the forecaster is used. It aims to predict long-term technical and social trends for which there is no historical data or history to indicate the impact of.

Cost of data collection methods

Cost in terms of software, time, paying for secondary data, primary data research etc vary with the method used. Such costs must be balanced against the benefits received if rational decisions regarding the usefulness of the forecasts are to be reached.

Activity

1   **Types of evidence** – What would you accept as evidence?

Imagine that you are thinking of investing in a small company called JMG Ltd. One day you meet an employee of the company in a bar, she says that the company is doing well these days.

(a) Would you accept her evidence as a reliable forecast and invest in the company?

(b) If she turned out to work for the corporate planning section, would you be more impressed?

(c) If you saw a graph of the company's shares over the last ten years and it showed an erratic but definite downward trend, then would you invest in the company?

(d) Assume that you have heard of a favourable research project, conducted by a Master's degree student, would this influence you?

(e) Finally, if you had seen a favourable newspaper report on the company, would that convince you?

Adapted from Metcalfe, p30.

2   How would you collect information to forecast the following?

(a) A restaurant proprietor wants to forecast the demand for kosher food in Adelaide for the next five years.

(b) A paint manufacturer has developed a paint that changes shades according to the amount of light that falls on it. As light increases it becomes darker, as light diminishes it becomes lighter. The manufacturer would like to determine the future demand for its product.

(c) The Adelaide Institute of TAFE is analysing its environment, it would like to predict student intakes for the next five years in Management Studies.

3   Look for secondary sources of information on the following:

(a) The numbers of overseas students currently enrolled at the Adelaide Institute of TAFE for the last three years.

(b) The growth in the consumer price index (inflation rate) in South Australia for the last five years.

(c) The market price of BHP shares for the last five days.

Qualitative methods

Quantitative methods are very useful for the short to medium forecasts, but they are less relevant for predicting the very long term. If you want to predict what products will be sold in the next month or the next two years, you consult a forecaster or statistician to apply a mathematical technique. If, however, you want to predict what products will be selling in what quantities in twenty years time or the technical trends in an industry, you would consult experts, the relevant areas of research and development or marketing analysis.

Qualitative methods need to be used where new paradigms are likely to occur or where technological and social change occurs.

The rate of change in some industries may be rapid so it is very difficult to predict anything beyond a few months.

1. Judgemental extrapolation

This is the method of visually inspecting a graph of a series to guess future movements with some accuracy. The advantage of this method is that it requires minimal expenditure of time, effort or money. This method is criticised as it does not lead to evidence that is particularly accurate nor is it a substitute for formal quantitative methods.

2. Expert judgement

Jury of executive opinion

These consist of forecasts of the quantity or event, such as the future technical developments or demands for a product, emerge from discussions at a meeting of a group or jury of corporate executive.

"The essential elements of this approach are:

1   The jury is composed of several individuals from different areas of corporate responsibility and therefore with different types of expertise and knowledge. The group therefore has available inputs from executives in marketing, finance, production, research and development and so on.

2   The final verdict emerges in some way following face-to-face discussions among the jury member, with each interpretation and weighing the view of the others in a quite informal way. The eventual forecast then might be regarded as resulting from a synthesis of the expert judgements of the individuals in the group."

"The precise mechanism through which the final forecast is achieved varies somewhat from one corporation to another, and perhaps also from one application to another. One possibility is that following the discussions, individual jury members write down their own forecasts, which are then averaged. Alternatively, a consensus forecast may be arrived at through more extensive discussions."

Newbold & Bos, p 480.

The advantage of the jury of opinion is its simplicity though it can be an expensive use of executive time. Another advantage is that it is a practical way to draw out knowledge that only lies in the minds of corporate executives.

Drawbacks are based on the informal or subjective nature of the process, the problem of personalities, power and politics that may prevent equitable and open discussions.

Selection Tree for Forecasting Methods

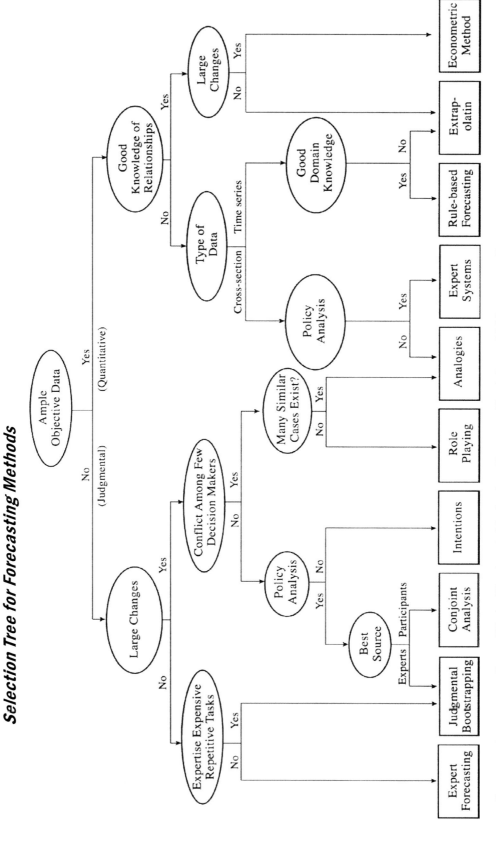

Source : Armstrong, Scott "Role Playing:A Method to Forecast Decisions, 1999, see readings.

3. Sales force composite forecasts

This is simply utilising the sales force knowledge and insights of customers via questionnaires or surveys. This information from the sales force is aggregated to form composite predictions over the region or country. The worth of this method depends on the accuracy of individuals.

The advantages of the sales force composite approach is that it uses the information from those closest to the customers. However, the drawback is that there is a tendency for optimism among the salespeople and they are often blind to changing paradigms.

4. Surveys

Surveys of suppliers, customers, employees or the public can be conducted to determine future trends. Questionnaires by mail, telephone or personal interviews can provide valuable insight into new markets, changing purchasing patterns and perceptions etc. If done in-house these can be done economically but use of specialist market research companies can be both time-consuming and expensive.

5. Nominal group technique

The nominal group restricts discussion during the decision making process, hence the term nominal group technique. Group members are all physically present, as in a traditional committee meeting, except the members are required to operate independently. Specifically, the following steps take place:

> **Nominal group technique:** A group decision-making technique in which members are present but operate interdependently

a. Members meet as a group; but before any discussion takes place, each member independently writes down his or her ideas on the problem.

b. This silent period is followed by each member presenting one idea to the group. Each member takes his or her turn, going around the table, presenting a single idea until all ideas have been presented and recorded (typically on a flip chart or chalkboard). No discussion takes place until all ideas have been recorded.

c. The group now discusses the ideas for clarity and evaluate them.

d. Each group member silently and independently assigns a rank to the ideas. The final decision is determined by the idea with the highest aggregate ranking.

The chief advantage of this technique is that it permits the group to meet formally but does not restrict independent thinking as so often happens in the traditional interacting group.

6.   Delphi technique

A more complex and time-consuming alternative is the Delphi technique, which is similar to the nominal group except that it does not require the physical presence of the group members. This is because the Delphi technique never allows the group members to meet face-to-face. The following steps characterise the Delphi technique:

> Delphi technique:
> A group decision-
> making technique
> in which
> members never
> meet face-to-
> face.

e.   The problem is identified and members are asked to provide potential solutions through a series of carefully designed questionnaires.

f.   Each member anonymously and independently completes the first questionnaire.

g.   Results of the first questionnaire are compiled at a central location, transcribed and reproduced.

h.   Each member receives a copy of the results.

i.   After viewing the results, members are again asked for their solutions. The results typically trigger new solutions or cause changes in the original position.

j.   Steps 4 and 5 are repeated as often as necessary until consensus is reached.

Like the nominal group technique, the Delphi technique insulates group members from the undue influence of others. It also does not require the physical presence of the participants. So, for instance, Minolta could use the technique to query its sales managers in Tokyo, Melbourne, Hong Kong, Paris, London, New York, Toronto and Auckland as to the best worldwide price for one of the company's new cameras. The cost of bringing the executives together at a central location is avoided, yet input is obtained from Minolta's major markets. Of course, the Delphi technique has its drawbacks. The method is extremely time-consuming. It is frequently not applicable when a speedy decision is necessary. Further, the method may not develop the rich array of alternatives that the interacting or nominal groups do. The ideas that might surface from the heat of face-to-face interaction may never arise.

7.   Role Playing

Role-playing is a method used to determine the impact of a forecast event on an organisation, its customers, suppliers etc. For example, a group of people can take on the role of doctor, nurse, patient representative, hospital administrator etc and they can take on these roles to determine the impact of a change in surgical technique that allows a previous five day stay in hospital to a one day visit to a day surgery.

"Active role playing is the preferred method for predicting decisions in situations in which parties interact. It is especially useful when:

- A small number of parties interact,
- Thay are in conflict,
- The conflicts involve large changes in the situation
- Little information exists about similar events in the past."

p17 Armstrong, Scott 'Role Playing: A Method to Forecast Decisions'
Principles of Forecasting: A handbook for Researchers and Practitioners,
Kluwer Academic Publishers, 1999.

The Benefits and Disadvantages Associated with Qualitative Forecasts

The Delphi Method

+ Experts are not brought together to discuss their views. The experts can contribute immune to groupthink.

+ Participants remain anonymous. Political or organisational pressure cannot be brought to bear.

+ Opportunity for revision of original forecasts as the process progresses.

+ Creativity cannot be governed or stifled.

+ Geographical location is not necessarily a restriction. Sources of ideas can be countries apart, but collated centrally.

+ Avoids the cost of travel and accommodation for participants.

- Can be slow to produce results. Not suitable where a quick decision is necessary.

- Participants may be restricted for ideas without group/social interaction. Isolation may support apathy.

La Prospective/Scenarios

+ A number of futures must be considered and decisions and actions considered that do not inhibit further choice.

+ Inflexible or irreversible decisions are recognised and avoided to prevent problems if forecasts turn out wrong.

+ Major environmental variable are weighed heavily, as is the division of counter strategies and the formulation of alternative scenarios.

- Complex and time consuming if executed completely.

- May prove expensive.

- Not suitable for a quick decision.

The Jury of Executive Opinion

+ The group is able to feed off the face to face interaction. The social group aspect may provide energy.

+ It may be relatively cheap to operate, if the organisation only uses executives from within a country, a city or single site.

+ The jury should contain a wide variety of company stakeholders, all experts, with functionally unique perspectives.

+ It may produce timely, rapid decisions by comparison to other techniques.

- Power and group personality factors may influence the outcome.

- Group think may occur, the executives may reach agreement based on cohesion and not on realistic appraisal.

- "Esteem Needs" that could be demonstrated by a high percentage of the group, could cause lengthy resolution if disagreement was to occur.

Judgemental Extrapolation

+ Minimal time, effort and money invested.

+ Requires few participants.

- Accuracy may be questionable.

Sales Force Composite

+ Information is gained from those closest to the customer.

+ If the customer was considered to be the major stakeholder in the sales chain, then the information passes on could be viewed as real (void of organisational or departmental bias).

- May be costly and time consuming.

- Undue optimism may be demonstrated by salespeople.

- Sales people may be unaware of shifting paradigms.

- Salespeople may lack understanding of broader environmental forces.

- May display similar negatives to the jury of executive opinion.

Nominal Group Technique

+ Task orientated, makes efficient use of time/resource.

+ Depersonalised, contributions become group property.

+ Cohesion and purpose are quickly achieved.

+ Balanced participation from all participants.

+ Encourages creative/innovative thinking.

+ Equal weight for all votes/contributions from all participants.

+ Authorities influence is restricted (organisational structure).

+   Structure provides format for closure.

-    Thorough preparation and education of participants may be difficult leading up to exercise.

-    May deny flow on information, the defining nature of the technique may stifle spin of ideas.

-    Difficult to apply to more than one issue.

-    May produce slow results.

-    Requires a skilled facilitator and detailed preplanning.

-    Could provide difficult to manage if comes too drawn out. Groups involved in lengthy sessions may find it difficult to stick to the rigid structure of the technique.

-    May prove expensive if senior managers/executives are used and a solution is slow to achieve.

Role Playing

+   Effective for situations in which a few parties interact.

+   Useful when the parties are in conflict.

+   Useful in predicting in situations that involve large changes.

+   Encourages creative/innovative thinking.

-    Requires a skilled facilitator and detailed preplanning.

Summary

Forecasts by experts are often inferior to those generated from simple quantitative methods, particularly for short-term forecasts. Problems in particular:

- When forecasts are prepared internally or within a "group think" there is a tendency to bias.

- Individuals appear to exhibit more certainty than is warranted about these predictions.

- They are not consistently accurate over time.

- It takes years of experience for someone to learn how to convert intuitive judgements into good forecasts.

UNIT 6

FORECASTING: QUANTITATIVE METHODS

Quantitative Methods

Managing data

Quantitative methods require data. It is necessary to obtain that data from primary or secondary sources, in order to make the forecast. Collecting the data means taking an original series, examining it and applying suitable adjustments to it so that it is in a good shape for analysis. The data that is used most often in forecasting are time series.

There is a process to implement quantitative methods.

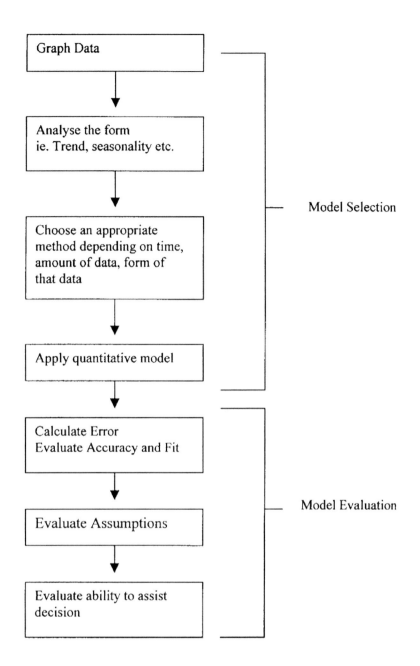

A time series chronological sequence of observations on a particular variable or a quantitative observation of some variable taken over time (usually hourly, daily, weekly, monthly, quarterly or yearly observations). Most of the forecasting methods will be based on time series as we are forecasting the future.

The first step in forecasting using quantitative methods is to examine the data by graphing it. Because a time series is a set of observations of a variable over time we can easily plot the time series for a visual picture of the past history of the variable. Usually time is on the horizontal axis and the units of measure for the variable of interest are on the vertical axis.

Principles of graph construction

Graph construction is in many ways an art. However, there are a number of basic principles to be observed if the graph is to be a good one. These are given below.

1. **The correct impression must be given**, since graphs depend upon visual interpretation, they are open to every trick in the field of optical illusion. Scale manipulation can considerably alter the impact of a graph, good (ie accurate, undistorted) presentation ensures that the correct impression is given.

2. **The graph must have a clear and comprehensive title.**

3. **The independent variable should always be placed on the horizontal axis.** Careful examination will generally show that the figures relating to one variable would be quite unaffected by changes in the other variable. The variable that will not be affected is called the independent variable and should be placed on the horizontal axis. Note that chronological time is always the independent variable and so is always on the horizontal axis.

4. **The vertical scale usually starts at zero.**

5. **Axes should be clearly labelled.** Labels should clearly state both (a) the variable and (b) the units 'Distance' and 'kilometres', 'Sales' and '$', 'People viewing TV' and 'Thousands'. Curves must be distinct – the purpose of a graph is to emphasise pattern or trend. This means that curves must be distinct. If two or more curves are graphed there must be no possibility of the curves being confused. To avoid such a possibility colour can be used to distinguish the curves. Alternatively, curves may be depicted as different kinds of dotted lines. Where there are two or more curves it is important, of course, that it must be very clear which data each curve represents.

6. **The graph must not be overcrowded with curves.** Too many curves on a graph make it difficult to see the pattern formed by any one curve and the whole point of the graphical presentation is lost. How many is 'too many' depends on circumstances. If the curves are close together and intersect, the limit may easily be three or even two. Where they are all spaced and do not intersect, many more may be put on the same graph.

7. **The source of data must always be given.** The source of the graphed data must always be given so that the user of the graph can, if they wish, refer to the actual figures on which the graph is based.

Analyse the form

Once the data has been plotted on graph paper or on computer it needs to be analysed.

Time series data comes in many different forms:

- *Stationary data* – the data is horizontal, its variability is consistent and there is no obvious seasonal influences or extreme values.

- *Non-stationary data* – any data which is not stationary.

- *Discontinuous data* – occasionally a severe shock to the industry/market may occur, eg the oil price shock, the Asian currency crisis of 1998. This kind of data series can either be split into two parts (before and after). Each part would have to be analysed separately or via other methods.

- *Extreme values* – if data behaves well except for one or two values. These extreme values will often distort the analysis and so are either left out or are adjusted so that they fit with the other values.

- *Seasonality* – sometimes a time series will show seasonal changes that repeat from one year to the next, i.e. ice-cream sales go up and down with the season.

- *Cyclical data* – many series are affected by the economic cycle which goes up and down over several years, i.e. the building industry typically moves with the economic cycle.

- *Irregular data* – fluctuations that are not due to trend, seasonal or cyclical components (these are often called random fluctuations).

Time series forecasting

Look for patterns in the data and assume they will continue, including:

> **White noise** comes from engineering and is a series where there is no discernable structure or pattern to the data.

- Trend (T)

- Seasonality (S)

- Cycles (C)

- Random variations (White noise)

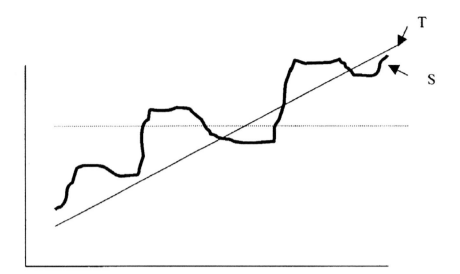

Activity

1. White noise is a purely random series, that is, it has virtually no discernible structure or pattern to it. Examples of white noise include:

    a. The winning numbers in the state lottery if recorded weekly.

    b. Suppose you stand on the street corner and record the number of licence plates of passing cars.

2. Do you think that any of the following provide examples of white noise series?

    a. The number of companies going bankrupt in a month.

    b. The daily changes in stock market prices.

    c. The number of runs scored by a baseball team in a sequence of consecutive games (goals scored by a soccer team, points scored by a basketball team, or whatever).

    d. The number of letters in succeeding words in a novel.

    e. The number of letters in the names of succeeding months (January = 7, February = 7, March = 5 etc).

    f. The total number of telephone calls made in a day in some developed country.

Quantitative methods in a snapshot

The most frequently used time series methods of forecasting are based on the notion of assigning weights to recent observations of the item to be forecast and then using the weighted sum of those observed (actual) values as the forecast. Much of the variety in available time series methods is simply due to the number of different approaches for determining the set of weights that will be applied.

Naive forecast

The simplest possible forecast measure assumes that the most recent data point provides the best prediction for subsequent points. For example, if the first four weeks sales for a year have been 23, 67, 52, 45 then the best forecast for week 5 is 45.

Moving average forecasts

Moving averages smooths the trend and uses the smoothed trend to forecast. You use the last three points averaged and use this for the forecast. For example, using the above example, the week 5 forecast using 3 monthly moving average is

$$= \quad 31 (67 + 52 + 45) = 55$$

The advantages of moving average forecasts are:

- you can ignore data that is "too" old
- it requires little data.

Disadvantage is that it lags behind any trend in the data. To avoid this you can try to weigh the more recent ("new") data over old data.

Moving average

Computer forecast using *n* most recent periods.

Moving Average

Compute forecast using *n* most recent periods

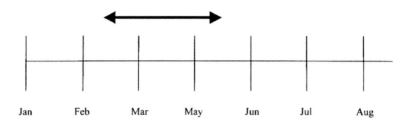

Jan   Feb   Mar   May   Jun   Jul   Aug

3 month Moving Avg:

June forecast:

$$F_{Jun} = (D_{Feb} + D_{Mar} + D_{May}) / 3$$

Moving Average

Example:

$$F_t = \sum_{i=t-n}^{t-1} D_i$$

Period	Demand	Forecast
1	10	10
2	12	11
3	14	12
4	15	13.7
5	16	15
6	17	16
7	19	17.3
8	21	19
9	23	21

The simple statistical method of moving averages will mimic some data better than complicated mathematical functions.

Mathematical Ability	Urgency of Preparatio	Amount of Data	Recommended Method

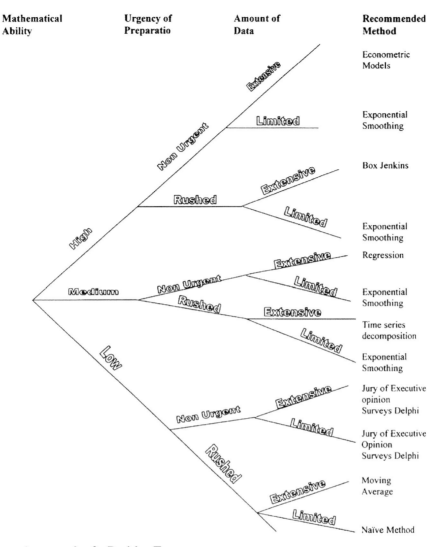

An example of a Decision Tree

Adapted from: 'Business Forecasting', Wilson & Keating, p435

If the time series is a stationary one, this may be the simplest and best method to use.

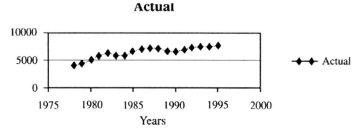

Actual

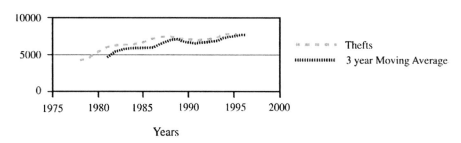

Three year Moving Average

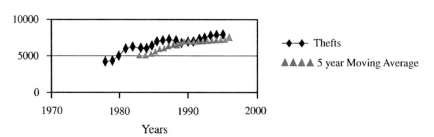

Five Year Moving Average

The choice of the interval for the moving average depends upon the length of the underlying cycle or pattern in the original data.

Exponential smoothing

Exponential smoothing is a procedure for continually revising a forecast in light of more recent experience

$$\hat{y}_{t+1} = \alpha y_t + (1-\alpha)\hat{y}_t \quad 0 \le \alpha \le 1$$

Exponential smoothing is simply the old forecast ($\hat{y}_t$) plus a times the error ($y_t - \hat{y}_t$) in the old forecast.

$\hat{y}_{t+1}$ is the forecast for the next period and is based on the smoothing constant multiplied by the actual for the current period (t) plus one minus the smoothing constant multiplied by the forecast for current period.

The smoothing constant α serves as the weighting factor. The actual value of α determines the extent to which the most current observation is to influence the forecast value. When α is close to 1 the new forecast will include substantial adjustment for any forecast error that occurred in the preceding forecast. Conversely, when α is close to 0 the new forecast will be very similar to the old one.

There are different ways of estimating α. One method of estimating is by an iterative procedure that minimises the mean squared error (MSE). The forecasts are computed for a number of a and the sum of the squared forecast errors is calculated for each. The value of α producing the smallest error is chosen for use in generating future forecasts.

In practice, a smoothing constant of between 0.1 and 0.3 works very well in most exponential smoothing forecasts.

The advantage of this method is that it is easy to use and works well with stationary data. However, data with a trend, it works poorly.

Exponential smoothing

- Smoothing constant between 0.1 – 0.3
- Easier to compute than moving average
- Most widely used forecasting method because of its easy use
- If no trend, all do equally well
- With trend, all do equally poorly.

Regression models (least-square method)

This statistical tool allows us to estimate the mathematical relationship between a dependent variable (Y) and a single independent variable (X). The dependent variable is the variable for which we want to develop a forecast.

The equation for a Linear Function is:

Y   = a + bX = e
a   = intercept with Y
        when X = 0
b   = is the slope of the line
E   = error term

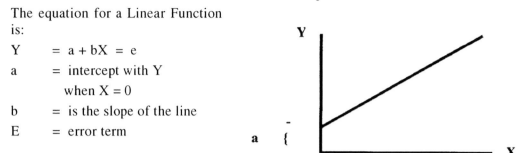

Historical analysts visually interpreted the data, nowadays computers do a far superior task. However, it is still important to graph the data as they allow additional information about the data pattern. It also allows inspection of the data to identify trend, seasonal and cyclical components, as well as data that doesn't fit the general pattern.

The estimation of the regression line can be done mathematically using the following least square equation.

$$a = \bar{Y} - b\bar{X} \qquad \text{or} \qquad \frac{\Sigma y - b\Sigma x}{N}$$

N =. Number of observations

$$b = \frac{N\Sigma xy - \Sigma x\Sigma y}{N\Sigma x^2 - (\Sigma x)^2}$$

Correlation coefficient

Correlation is concerned with the relationship between variables. If there is a relationship then the movement in one variable (time) will cause a movement of the other variable. It is important that there is a relationship between two variables for regression analysis to work. Therefore it is necessary to test your data for the degree of this correlation.

The Correlation Coefficient (Pearson product correlation coefficient) needs to be close to +1 or –1 for there to be a good relationship, conversely the result near 0 implies minimal relationship.

$$r = \frac{N\Sigma xy - (\Sigma x)(\Sigma y)}{\sqrt{[N\Sigma x^2 - (\Sigma x^2)][N\Sigma y^2 - (\Sigma y)^2]}}$$

or

$$r = \frac{\Sigma(x - \bar{x})(y - \bar{y})}{\sqrt{\Sigma(x - \bar{x})^2 \Sigma(y - \bar{y})^2}}$$

$\bar{x}$ = mean of x = $\dfrac{\text{sum of values } (\Sigma x)}{\text{number of values } (N)}$

$\bar{y}$ = mean of y = $\dfrac{\text{sum of values } (\Sigma y)}{\text{number of values } (N)}$

r = Correlation Coefficient

Calculation of the correlation coefficient (r)

Example: From given data, identify any correlation.

Calculate and describe the correlation coefficient between advertising (x) and sales (y)		
Year	$'000 Advertising	$'000 sales
1990	10	200
1991	11	230
1992	12	250
1993	14	270
1994	15	280
1995	16	300

Solution

Adv x	Sales y	$\lvert x - \bar{x} \rvert$	$\lvert y - \bar{y} \rvert$	$(x - \bar{x})(y - \bar{y})$	$(x - \bar{x})^2$	$(y - \bar{y})^2$

Forecasting using the regression method requires the following steps:

1. Plot data on a graph.

2. Calculate the correlation coefficient to determine whether there is a relationship between the variables.

3. Calculate the line of best fit by:

   - Visually (tends to be very inaccurate)

   - Use the equations

   - Use computer generated results.

4. Calculate the regression data using X values.

5. Forecast using the next X values.

6. Plot all onto a graph.

   (see readings for example)

Using a casual regression model to forecast

This is similar to regression except that a change in the independent variable (X) is assumed to cause a change in the dependent variable (Y) (and this variable is not time). The selection of an appropriate casual variable (X) should be based on some insight that suggests that a casual relationship is reasonable.

Car sales: potential casual variables might be:

Income	Interest rates
New-car prices	Unemployment rates
Employment	Used car prices
Gasoline prices	Savings

It is important that the independent variable be selected on the basis of a logical construct that relates it to be the dependent variable, ie there is a logical reason for the movement in one to create or respond to movement of the other variable.

Ways to test the relationship is to plot the two variables on the same graph as a time series and/or to calculate the correlation coefficient. This can also help us see if there is a consistency over time.

If the slope of the regression line is zero (horizontal) then there may be no statistical relationship between X and Y or if the correlation coefficient is near 0 then there is minimal relationship.

Linear regression

Look for a linear relationship between X and Y:

$\hat{y} = a + bx$

$\hat{y}$ = Quantity to be estimated

a = intercept of Y

b = slope of increase in Y

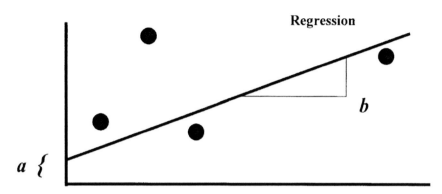

Box-Jenkins (ARIMA)

The Box-Jenkins methodology is a technically sophisticated way of forecasting a variable by looking only at the post pattern of the time series.

The Box-Jenkins uses the most recent observation as a starting value and proceeds to analyse recent forecasting errors to select the most appropriate adjustment for future time periods.

The Box-Jenkins process is best suited to longer range rather than shorter range forecasting.

In Box-Jenkins methodology we start with the observed time series itself and examine its characteristics in order to get an idea of what black box we might use to transform the series into white noise. (White noise is essentially a purely random series of numbers, ie when there is not a relationship between consecutive observed values and the previous value will be no help in predicting future values, eg lottery).

We begin by trying the most likely of many black boxes, and if we get white noise, we assume that there is the "correct" model to use in generating forecasts of the series.

When choosing the "correct" black box there are three types of models:

1.   Moving average models

2.   Autoregressive models

3.   Mixed autoregressive – moving average models.

Comparison of standard regression analysis and Box-Jenkins methodology

For standard regression analysis:

1. Specify the casual variables

2. Use a linear (or other) regression model

3. Estimate the constant and slope coefficients

4. Examine the summary statistics and try other model specifications

5. Choose the most desirable model specification (perhaps on the basis of RMSE).

Start here:

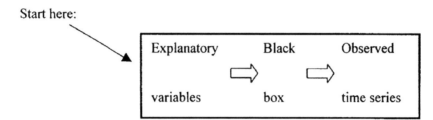

For Box-Jenkins methodology:

1. Start with the observed time series

2. Pass the observed time series through a black box

3. Examine the time series that results from passage through the black box

4. If the black box is correctly specified, only white noise should remain

5. If the remaining series is not white noise, try another black box.

Start here:

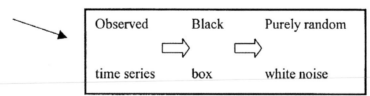

Time series decomposition

The information provided by time-series decomposition is consistent with the way managers tend to look at data and often helps them to get a better handle on data movement by providing concrete measurements for factors that are otherwise not qualified.

p 264 Wilson & Keating.

Time-series decomposition models can be used to identify components by breaking the series into its component parts and then reassembling the parts to construct a forecast.

The popularity is due primarily to three factors:

1.   They provide excellent forecasts.

2.   Easy to understand and to explain to forecast users, therefore they are likely to be correctly interpreted and used.

3.   They are consistent with the way managers tend to look at data and often help them to get a better handle on data movements.

Classical time-series decomposition

Time series = Pattern + Residuals

Patterns are variations around:

- Trend (T)
- Cyclical (C)
- Seasonal (S)
- Irregular (I)

The residuals are random data.

You can use either of these models:

1. $Y = T + C + S + I$

2. $Y = T \times C \times S \times I$

or they can be of a mixed component

3. $Y = (T \times C \times S) + I$

The task is to find the components contained in our time series, then to separate them out (i.e. decompose the series, by taking out the trends and flattening the irregular movements. You then use the flattened and trend less figures to make a forecast then you add back into the forecast the trends you had taken out of the original time series.

If we use No 3, then if you divide the time series with the calculated trend values of this time series we obtain the following:

$$\frac{T \times C \times I}{T} \quad = \quad C \times I$$

This works well when the seasonal factors are weak, but the cyclical influence is strong.

To get rid of the irregular variations you can use moving averages or regression.

Moving averages of **C x I**   = C

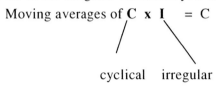

cyclical   irregular

The next step is to change this unpredictable variation into a regular and typical variation.

See reading for examples.

To do a time series decomposition you can undertake the following steps:

1. Graph actual data
2. Determine seasonal index
    - find the average for each period (month/quarter)
    - the seasonal index is then calculated by determining each respective periods average in proportion to the mean average of all data periods, ie mean of June is divided by the mean average of all data
3. Multiply data by 100/index to find deseasonalised data.
4. Forecast using either naive, exponential smoothing, moving average or regression.
5. Put back seasonal effect by multiplying forecast by appropriate index.
6. Graph forecast, deseasonal data and original data.

Transformations

Curve	Formula	Transformation
1. Straight line (linear)	$Y = a + bx$	First differences constant
2. Parabola	$Y = a + bx + cx^2$	Second differences constant
3. Third degree parabola	$Y = a + bx + cx^2 + dx^3$	Third differences constant
4. Hyperbola	$Y = {}^a/_x$	First differences of reciprocal logs are constant
5. Exponential curve	$Y + a^{bx}$	First differences of reciprocal logs are constant
6. Modified exponential	$Y = k + ab^x$	First differences are declining at a constant percentage
7. Compertz curve	$Y = ka^{bx}$	Growth of first differences logs is declining at a constant percentage
8. Logistic curve	$^1/_Y = k + ab^x$	First differences of reciprocal values are declining at a constant percentage

A series can be transformed into a stable/stationary data by transforming the series, eg by taking logarithms, square roots or difference etc. Once the data has been transformed, then simple techniques such as naïve, moving average or simple exponential smoothing can be used.

Evaluation of forecasts

Evaluating forecasts

It is important that you evaluate the quality of forecasts. Given the considerable amounts of money, time and effort are expanded in the production of the forecast and its purpose is to assist in making business decisions, where the potential losses or gains can be substantial, you want to ensure that the forecast is accurate.

It is easy to focus on forecast methodology, its sophistication and complexity, but the real issue is how good is the forecast's performance and how well will it produce real forecasts.

The forecast needs to conform to various criteria for it to provide a quality forecast:

- **Objectivity** – A forecast is objective if the result of the forecasting process depends entirely on the data, not the person conducting the forecast.

- **Validity** – A forecast is valid if it approximates the series that we are interested in (i.e. there is high correlation between them).

- **Reliability** – A forecast is reliable if there is consistency in the results produced by it.

- **Accuracy** – A forecast is accurate if it is valid and has a good fit.

- **Confidence** – This indicates the probability with which we should accept the results. This is measured by confidence intervals.

- **Sensitivity** – The more scattered the results of a method are the more sensitive the method is.

"To summarise, we can say that we should be pleased with our results if we use a sensitive and reliable method, which is producing valid and accurate forecasts, which are placed within an acceptable narrow confidence interval."

p147 Pecar.

Many companies do not evaluate the quality of their forecasts. However, the simple rule applies – nothing improves until you start to measure it. An objective measurement of forecast quality should be established to help improve forecast quality and also to plan for some contingency (may be safety stock) against the potential forecast error.

Forecast tracking

Forecast tracking is a means of keeping tabs on how well actual observations follow forecasted values by:

Applying judgement rules. When do forecast errors exceed average period-to-period changes, are errors consistently in the same direction, are errors too great. Use of confidence intervals.

1.   Forecast error

The forecast error is the difference between the actual and the forecast observations.

$$e_t = X_t - \hat{X}_t$$

X_t = actual observation in the original series in the period t

$\hat{X}_t$ = forecast for the period t

The forecast error (e_t) should be random or irregular if the forecast is really representing the original series. If there is a pattern to the e_t then the forecast is not producing a good result.

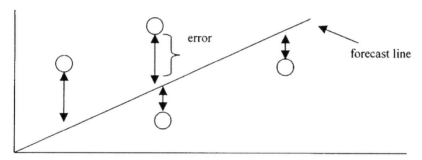

There are a number of ways of measuring forecast accuracy. These are all based on measuring the error between the actual data and the fitted data.

Mean Absolute Deviation (MAD)

$$= \quad \frac{\sum_{i=1} |e_t|}{n} = \frac{\sum_{i=1} |Y_i -- \hat{Y}_i|}{n}$$

$$= \frac{\sum |\text{Forecast Errors}|}{n}$$

Root Mean Squared Error (RMSE)

$$= \sqrt{\frac{(\sum_{i=1} |e_t^2|)}{n}}$$

Mean Absolute Percentage Error (MAPE)

$$= \frac{\sum_{i=1}(|e|Yt) \times 100}{n}$$

You are usually able to apply several quantitative forecasting methods to your data. By calculating the error using the above you can compare one to the other. For example, the one with the lowest RMSE will produce the most accurate forecast.

Computing MAD, RMSD

Per	Dem	Exp Sm	Error	Abs Val	Squared
1	10	10			
2	12	10			
3	14	10.6			
4	15	11.6			
5	16	12.6			
6	17	13.6			
7	19	14.7			
8	21	16.0			
9	23	17.5			
Sum					

Steps for Choosing the Best Quantitative Forecasting Method

- Plot the data on a graph
- Look at the plotted data and make a preliminary visual assessment as to whether or not the following time series components are present
  - Trend
  - Season
  - Cycle
- Based on the preliminary assessment of the plotted data, determine which method is most likely to be effective.
- Find MAD for chosen method

- Because no forecasting method is perfect, it is advisable to use one or two methods that are reasonably suited to the data and find MAD for them too.

- Choose forecast from method with best MAD

- Graph forecast data versus original time series data.

2. Confidence intervals

We can create an interval around our forecast which will indicate the probability that our forecast estimates the actual. Using the error between the forecast and the actual for the population will give an indication of the confidence interval for the new forecast.

> 95% confidence interval
> forecast estimate $\pm$ 1.96 (error)
> 90% confidence interval
> forecast estimate $\pm$ 1.645 (error)
> 99% confidence interval
> forecast estimate $\pm$ 2.58 (error)

Combining forecast / Use of Multiple Methods

"It was found that 83% of expert forecasters believe that combining forecasts will produce more accurate forecasts than could be obtained from individual methods."

Fred Collopy & J Scott Armstrong, Expert Opinions about Extrapolation and the Mystery of Overlooked Discontinuities, International Journal of Forecasting 8, No 4, December 1992, pp575–82.

Previously we have looked at methods for obtaining or determining the best forecasting method. Evidence has proven that a more accurate forecast can be obtained by combining separate predictions.

The forecaster can combine very different types of quantitative models so that:

1. The different forecast models extract different predictive factors from essentially the same data.

2. That the different models offer different predictions because they use different variables.

Source: Business Forecasting, Wilson & Keating, p391.

A developing branch of forecasting involves the use of multiple methods to produce the final forecasts. An issue of the International Journal of Forecasting contained a special section on this new technique. Portions of the abstracts of three articles in the issue illustrate the developing nature of the use of multiple methods:

- Research from over 200 studies demonstrates that the use of multiple methods produces consistent by modest gains in accuracy.

- The amount of research on the use of multiple methods is substantial. Yet, relatively little is known about when and how managers use multiple methods. Important managerial issues that require further study include managerial adjustment of quantitative forecasts, the use of expert systems in using multiple methods, and analyses of the cost using multiple methods.

- Considerable literature has accumulated over the years regarding the use of multiple methods. The primary conclusion of this line of research is that forecast accuracy can be substantially improved through the use of multiple methods.

In the coming years, further research will likely be conducted on the advantages of the use of multiple methods, along with the techniques for doing so. The objective of using multiple methods will be to develop accurate forecasts that are cost effective.

John & Arthur, 1995, p525 Business Forecasting, Prentice Hall,
Englewood Cliffs.

The combined forecasts should therefore result in reduced forecast error.

There are also sophisticated methods of combining forecasts that weigh each forecast to improve its accuracy. This is beyond the expectations of this course.

Why try to forecast?

"It is far better to foresee even without certainty than not to foresee at all."

Henri Poincare in The Foundations of Science, p129.

A pragmatic remark from one of the foundation builders of chaos theory: Forecasting may not be 100% accurate but it can improve decision making for the following reasons:

- The power of forces such as economics, competition, markets, social concerns and ecological environment to affect the individual firm is severe and continues to grow.

- Forecast assessment is a major input in management's evaluation of different strategies at business decision-making levels.

- The inference of no forecasting is that the future either contains no significant change or there is ample time to react "over time".

> *"The forecaster's motto: Always Wrong but Never Uncertain".*

Arguments against forecasting

> *"By its very nature, forecasting is inaccurate, a bit of black magic . . . You're going to have your misses and you have to understand that it's not a fundamental failure. It's not like you screwed up or anything. A change in the plan of record is simply something you need to adapt to as a reality of doing business."*
>
> *Forecasting: Data, Technology and a bit of Black Magic, by Paul Human*
> *Electronic Buyers' News, Feb 12, 1996, Issue: 933.*

> *"Better to slay the forecasting beast than let ever-unreliable forecasts kill your business."*
>
> *The Death of Forecasting, Blair R Williams, OEM Magazine, Jan 10,*
> *1997, Issue 535.*

The bad feelings for forecasting are in part attributed to:

- bad experience
- speculations of journalists, extreme claims and sensation seekers
- discounting forecasting methodology.

These views can be summarised in three quotes provided by D B Stephenson, www.cict.fr/lsp/Stephen/STATS:

> *"Forecasting future events is often like searching for a black cat in an unlit room, that may not even be there."*
>
> *Steve Davidson in The Crystal Ball.*

Future events, like cats, can prove to be elusive!

> *"Wall Street indices predicted nine out of the last five recessions!"*
>
> *Paul A Samuelson in Newsweek, Science and Stocks, 19 Sept 1966.*

False alarms are an embarrassing subject for those involved in prediction.

> *"He who lives by the crystal ball soon learns to eat ground glass."*
>
> *Edgar R Fiedler in The Three Rs of Economic Forecasting – Irrational,*
> *Irrelevant and Irreverent, June 1977.*

A cautionary career note based on past experience.

How to communicate forecasts

'Objective analysis versus biased implementers and coordinator.'

Forecasting is in the interface between art and science. Forecasters are required to give opinions. Forecasters need input from people and be able to work and manage the process.

1. Purpose or usefulness of the forecast (including its timeframe).

2. Key underlying assumptions.

3. Input data.

4. Forecast numbers themselves.

5. Graphic display of history with the forecasts.

6. Any other comments placing the forecasts in the proper perspective.

7. Reporting on the past forecasting performance record.

Other useful application concepts

1. The 'Parsimony' principle, always choose the simple over the complex, if things are equivalent.

2. Forecasts must be revised periodically as time brings horizons closer and conditions change. This activity includes the need for detection of errors and for incremental corrections to improve understanding of underlying relationships.

3. It is desirable to have centralised source for data within the organisation.

4. The forecaster quest for a Holy Grail is to search for those key factors that are truly sensitive – to search for patterns of experience in one's own company and industry.

5. Forecasting should not be viewed as an answer or a decision but rather as one more input for decision making in managerial work.

Nine Golden Rules

Below are nine golden rules that can assist you in your forecast. These are provided by (source: *http://www.mfgmagic.com.au/*) Manufacturing Magic, 1997.

Most manufacturing businesses need to forecast future demands for their products. At an operational level these forecasts are used to:

- maintain inventories of finished products
- plan for replenishment of raw materials and other items
- plan for production and capacity.

Unfortunately most companies are struggling to develop accurate forecasts and this issue often creates friction between the sales/marketing group and the planning/manufacturing group in many companies. Although we haven't got a magic wand to help you develop 100% accurate forecasts, we can list here a few often forgotten principles/rules/suggestions on forecasting.

1. Forecasts are always wrong

The truth remains – no one can forecast with 100% accuracy. The trick is to establish your targets for forecast accuracy for the various products/product groups you need to forecast and work to achieve those targets.

2. Forecast accuracy must be measured

Many companies do not measure accuracy of their forecasts. You know the very simple rule – nothing gets improved until you start measuring it. An objective measurement of forecast accuracy should be established to help improve forecast accuracy and also to potential forecast error.

3. Use aggregate forecasts where you can

Aggregate forecasts are likely to be more accurate than detailed forecasts (for example, forecast of total number of Panadol tablets that will be sold is likely to be more accurate than the forecast of how many '12, 24, 50, 100, 500 packs' of Panadol will be sold). Hence, examine how forecasts are really used and where you can use aggregate forecasts instead of detailed forecasts.

4. The further out you forecast, less accurate the forecast will be

However, as a minimum, you need to forecast demands for any product to cover its cumulative lead time and if you import raw materials, the cumulative lead time can easily add up to 3 to 6 months. However, have you ever considered ways of reducing your lead times? Reducing lead times will help you reduce the horizon over which you rely heavily on highly accurate forecasts resulting in more accurate plans.

5. Establish different demand streams

Depending upon situations, you may want to break your target markets into streams (eg major retailers, small shops, direct sales etc) and forecast for each stream/customer group separately.

Also you need to break your demand data into base sales and promotional sales. As a general rule, one should forecast base business and plan for promotional activities.

6.   Identify forecasting units/levels required

Marketing considers market segments they plan while sales considers categories they control. Both these functions prefer to plan in dollars while production elects to plan in units. Ultimately for planning purposes, you need to develop a forecast by product in units; however, your forecasting system should be flexible enough so that it can aggregate forecasts/actual demands to different levels of details in alternate units and in dollars. Always store the information at the lowest level and provide for the needed flexibility.

7.   Invest in a forecasting tool

It is amazing to me that many companies will employ highly intelligent, highly paid executives to spend their time gathering sales data for them to massage it in a Lotus or Excel Spreadsheet to develop a forecast – a process that takes a few days. More often than not they spend 95% of this time gathering data and 5% of the time in evaluating results.

8.   Make forecasting a process

Too many managers think that a solution to their forecasting problem is to buy a forecasting package, load in history and drop the calculated forecast into the Master Schedule. No matter how much you invest in your solution, the best any forecasting program can do is evaluate history and extrapolate into the future.

This should be considered just a starting point. An effective forecasting process must include:

a.   Analysis of items with low forecast accuracy

b.   Review of forecasts generated by any forecasting package

c.   Adjustments for special factors such as promotion and price changes

d.   Input from people as close to the ultimate customer as possible

e.   Documenting underlying forecasting assumptions

f.   An effective management review and communication step.

9.   Develop a common level of understanding

Do not make assumptions that everyone understands how forecasts are generated and used. It is important for all people involved in the forecasting process to clearly understand the whole process, where they fit in it and what their contribution does to the entire forecasting and planning process. This may require sound education and training, an area very often sadly and badly neglected.

Believe me, if you follow these time-proven Golden Rules, it is not difficult to implement a well-managed forecast process and the results from it will be very significant – Good Luck!

UNIT 7

FIVE FORCES

Porter's Five Competitive Forces Model

There are a number of ways to audit or analyse the environment. **Five Competitive Forces Model, Porter, M (1980)** utilises five competitive forces to analyse the nature and intensity of competition. This is different from the understanding of the external environment, which sets the context for the organisations future. Porter's model is about the relative power position in the industry. When using Porter's model, remember:

- It is about the future (we are not interested in the now or the past).

- It is about the power relationships, how strong you are within the five forces that contribute to competition in the industry. It is about how you can position your unit/organisation to increase its relative power.

- It is only useful if you can come to some conclusion and act on it. The analysis is only the tool to help you understand the industry and how you are positioned for the future. Its being able to extract the information to use that is important.

The five competitive forces are:

1   **Rivalry.** The extent to which competitors jockey for position with tactics as price competition, advertising battles, product introductions, or increased customer service or warranties. All these tactics lower profits for industry competitors by lowering prices charged or raising the costs of doing business.

2   The **bargaining power of customers** is the extent to which customers can force down prices, bargain for higher quality or more service at the same price and play competitors against each other. Customers tend to be powerful when quantities purchases are a large proportion of a seller's total sales, when products or services represent a significant portion of a customer's cost, or when items needed are standard to the industry. The greater customers' bargaining power, the lower profit potential is.

3   The **bargaining power of suppliers** is the extent to which suppliers can exert power by threats to raise prices or reduce the quality of goods and services provided. Suppliers are more powerful when there are few of them selling to many businesses in an industry, without substitutes for products or services, or when the products or services are critical inputs. The consequence is the greater the bargaining power of suppliers, the lower the industry profit potential.

4 The **threat of new entrants** is the degree to which new competitors can enter markets. New entrants bring added capacity and possibly substantial resources. This can result in price wars and/or increased costs for existing businesses, due to increased expenditures (such as added advertising, larger sales force, better service) to maintain market share. The threat of entry depends on the barriers to entry and the likely reactions to new entrants from existing competitors. High barriers to entry for a business exist when large capital investment is needed (eg the telecommunications industry), when established competitors have products or services customers see as unique (eg. a brand name perfume), or when economics of scale make it difficult for new entrants to build volume up (eg car manufacturing).

 When barriers are high and new entrants expect existing competitors to react vigorously the threat of new entrants is low. In contrast, when barriers are low and new entrants expect existing competitors to react mildly, then the new entrant threat is high and, consequently, the industry's profit potential low.

5 The **threat of substitute products or services** is the extent to which businesses in other industries offer substitute products. For example, artificial sweeteners substitute for sugar and electricity for natural gas in producing energy. The consequence is that substitutes reduce the industries profit potential.

Porter's model is an evolution from previous studies that have examined why some industries are more profitable than others.

Factors Influencing Average Industry Profitability

FACTOR	WILL LOWER PROFITABILITY	WILL RAISE PROFITABILITY
1. STRUCTURE OF COMPETITION	NUMEROUS / EQUAL SIZE	ONE DOMINANT
2. INDUSTRY GROWTH	SLOW	RAPID
3. DIFFERENTIATION	NEGLIGIBLE	SIGNIFICANT
4. FIXED COSTS	HIGH	LOW
5. CAPACITY INCREMENTS	LARGE	SMALL
6. EXIT BARRIERS	HIGH	LOW
7. DIVERSITY OF STRATEGY	SIGNIFICANT	LIMITED
8. EASE OF ENTRY	EASY	DIFFICULT
- SCALE THRESHOLDS		
- ACCESS TO DISTRIBUTION		
- COMMON TECHNOLOGY		
9. NUMBERS OF BUYERS	FEW	MANY
10. BUYER PURCHASING VOLUMES	LARGE	SMALL
11. BUYER PROFITABILITY	LOW	HIGH
12. BUYER PURCHASES IMPACT ON END-PRODUCT PERFORMANCE AND QUALITY	UNIMPORTANT	IMPORTANT
13. BUYER POTENTIAL TO BACK INTEGRATE	SIGNIFICANT	POSSIBLE
14. BUYER ABILITY TO SWITCH TO SUBSTITUTES OR OTHER SUPPLIERS	EASY	DIFFICULT
15. TIME TO BRING ON INCREASED CAPACITY		

ELEMENTS OF INDUSTRY STRUCTURE

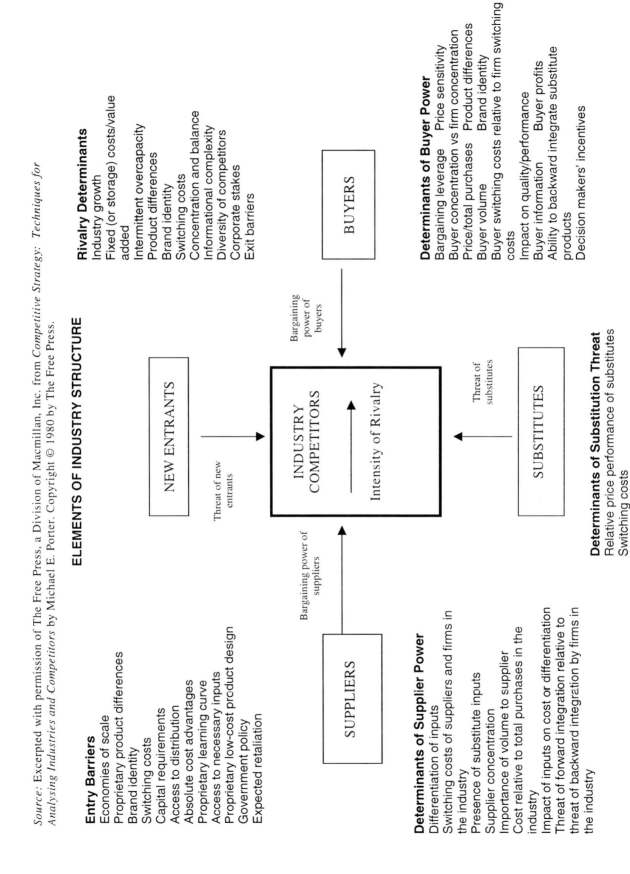

Entry Barriers
Economies of scale
Proprietary product differences
Brand identity
Switching costs
Capital requirements
Access to distribution
Absolute cost advantages
Proprietary learning curve
Access to necessary inputs
Proprietary low-cost product design
Government policy
Expected retaliation

Rivalry Determinants
Industry growth
Fixed (or storage) costs/value added
Intermittent overcapacity
Product differences
Brand identity
Switching costs
Concentration and balance
Informational complexity
Diversity of competitors
Corporate stakes
Exit barriers

Determinants of Buyer Power
Bargaining leverage   Price sensitivity
Buyer concentration vs firm concentration
Price/total purchases   Product differences
Buyer volume   Brand identity
Buyer switching costs relative to firm switching costs
Impact on quality/performance
Buyer information   Buyer profits
Ability to backward integrate substitute products
Decision makers' incentives

Determinants of Supplier Power
Differentiation of inputs
Switching costs of suppliers and firms in the industry
Presence of substitute inputs
Supplier concentration
Importance of volume to supplier
Cost relative to total purchases in the industry
Impact of inputs on cost or differentiation
Threat of forward integration relative to threat of backward integration by firms in the industry

Determinants of Substitution Threat
Relative price performance of substitutes
Switching costs
Buyer propensity to substitute

NEW ENTRANTS

Threat of new entrants

INDUSTRY COMPETITORS

Intensity of Rivalry

SUPPLIERS

Bargaining power of suppliers

BUYERS

Bargaining power of buyers

SUBSTITUTES

Threat of substitutes

Models that assist in the interpretation and analysis of the industry

Experience Curve

The experience curve describes the potential cost position for a well managed firm in the industry. It does not follow that all firms will be on it but with good management and hard work there is a particular decreasing cost/volume relationship that can be achieved. Just where any competitor sits on the curve is a function of how much experience it has, as well as its management competence. The result of this spread will generally be differences in profitability that are a function of differences in market share.

In some businesses there is an observed tendency for unit costs to decline as the firm gains more cumulative experience in producing a product. Costs decline because workers improve their methods and become more efficient (the classic learning curve), layout improves, specialised   equipment and processes are developed, better performance is coaxed from equipment, product design changes make manufacturing easier, techniques for measurement and control of operations improve and so on. These improvements can apply to distribution, marketing and logistics and other functions.

Experience can act as a barrier to other firms and affect the competitive ranking of firms.

The effect of the experience curve can be limited by:

- changes in technology, this may alter the production process or product fundamentally, i.e. new rules to the game
- product redesign
- cost components outside the control of the producer for example trade restrictions may stop supplies, or a drought may increase prives of raw materials

Why Do Costs Go Down With Experience?

The Experience Curve Effect Caused By:
- Learning curve effect
- Scale effect
  - ➤ equipment
  - ➤ distribution
  - ➤ overhead
  - ➤ purchasing
- Investment for cost reduction
- Yield improvements
- Substitution and displacement

The Experience Curve[1]

A large size, relative to competitors, can bring benefits. In particular, if a company has a market share substantially greater than its competitors it has opportunities to achieve greater profitability. Lower costs can be achieved if the company is well managed and takes advantage of opportunities offered by being larger. These lower costs can be passed on to the consumer in the form of lower prices, which in turn puts pressure on competitors' profit margins and strengthens the position of the market leader.

Lower costs are achieved through economies of scale and the experience or learning effect. In the 1960s the Boston Consulting Group in the USA estimated that the cost of production decreases by between 10% and 30% each time that a company's experience in producing the product or service doubles as long as the company is managed well. In other words, as cumulative production increases over time, there is a potential cost reduction at a predictable rate. The company learns how to do things better. The savings are spread across all value-added costs; manufacturing, administration, sales, marketing and distribution. In addition the cost of supplies decreases as suppliers experience the same learning benefits.

The experience effect has been observed in high and low technology industries, in new and mature industries, in both manufacturing and service businesses, and in relation to consumer and industrial markets. Specific examples are cars, semi-conductors, petrochemicals, long distance telephone calls, synthetic fibres, airline transportation, crushed limestone and the cost of administering life insurance.

The experience curve is illustrated by plotting on a graph the cumulative number of units over time (the horizontal axis) and the cost per unit (the vertical axis). Figure 1 below does this.

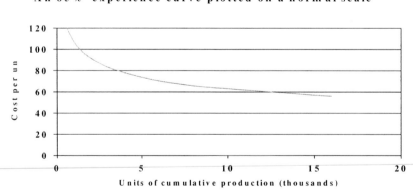

Figure 1
An 85% experience curve plotted on a normal scale

---

[1] Thompson, J.L.(1997) Strategic Management: Awareness and Change, 3rd edition, Thomson International. London.

This particular curve is called an '85% experience curve' as every time output is doubled the cost per unit falls to 85% of what it was. In reality the plot will be of a least squares line but the trend will be clear. However it is more common to plot the data on logarithmic scales on both axes, and this shows the straight line effect illustrated in Figure 2 below.

Figure 2:
The same 85% experience curve plotted in log-log form

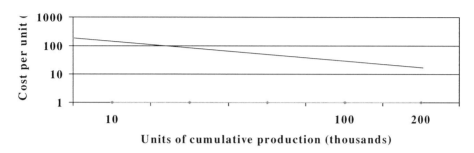

Sources of the experience effect

- Increased labour efficiency through learning and consequent skills improvement.

- The opportunity for greater specialisation in production methods

- Innovations in the production process

- Greater productivity from equipment as people learn how to use it more efficiently

- Improved resource mix as products are redesigned with cost savings in mind.

This is not an exhaustive list, and the savings will not occur naturally. They result from good management.

Pricing decisions and the experience effect

A market leader or other large producer who enjoys a cost advantage as a result of accumulated experience will use this as the basis for pricing strategy linked to his or her objectives, which might be profit or growth and market share oriented. Figure 3 illustrates one way that industry prices might be forced down (in real terms, after accounting for inflation) as the market leader benefits from lower costs.

Figure 3:
Pricing in relation to costs and the experience effect

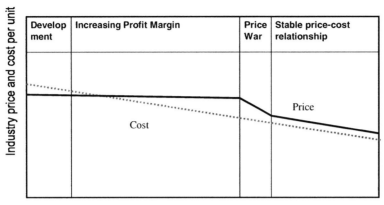

Cumulative industry production

Initially prices are below costs incurred because of the costs of development. As demand, sales and production increase prices fall, but at a slower rate than costs; the producer is enjoying a higher profit margin. This will be attractive to any competitors or potential competitors who feel they can compete at their price even if their costs are higher. If competition becomes intensive and the major producer(s) wish to assert authority over the market they will decrease prices quickly and force out manufacturers whose costs are substantially above theirs. Stability might be restored. Companies with large market shares can therefore dictate what happens in a market, but there is a need for caution. If a company ruthlessly chases a cost advantage via the experience effect the implication could be ever increasing efficiency as a result of less flexibility. The whole operating system is geared towards efficiency and cost savings. If demand changes or competitors innovate unexpectedly the strategy will have run out of time as we have already seen. Companies should ensure that they are flexible enough to respond.

Life cycles of products

Most products have a life cycle. Predictability products have a four staged lifecycle: introduction, growth, maturity and eventually decline. From introduction they move into a growth phase, then reach maturity and eventually decline. For some products this life cycle can be very rapid (remember Rubiks cubes?), while for others it may be long and drawn out (eg Hills Hoist).

Products show different characteristics at each stage in terms of sales, profit, capital investment, net cash flow and in term of competitors. By understanding where a product or group of products are on the lifecycle will assist in interpreting its competitive position and future prospects.

Product Life Cycle Characteristics and Responses

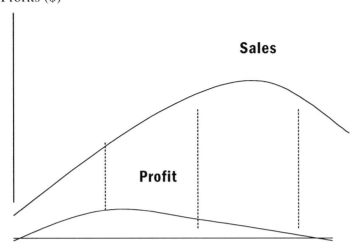

	Introduction	Growth	Maturity	Decline
Sales volume	Low	Fast growing	Stable	Declining
Profits	Negligible	Peak levels	Declining	Low
Competition	None	Increasing	Many competitors	Reducing
Product	Basic	Improving	Differentiated	Less variety
Customer	Innovator	Mass market	Mass market saturated	Laggards
Strategy	Expand market	Market penetration high	Defend – share falling	Productivity
Marketing Expenses	High	High – declining	Falling	Low
Marketing	Product awareness	Brand preference	Brand loyalty	Selective

	Introduction	Growth	Maturity	Decline
Profit Potential	Limited and patchy	High margins	Variable – increased competition as growth slows	Usually low – subject to industry structure
Customer Characteristics	'Early adopters', specialists	Widening market	Mass market	Knowledgeable and demanding customers
Key Success Factors	R & D, production challenges usually critical. Direct marketing and distribution common	A scramble for market share and leadership – advertising and distribution become key factors	A search for adding value and new niche markets – differenti-ation	Emphasis on cost reduction and efficiency to improve margins

Bruce R (2000) **Creating Your Own Strategic Future**, *Harper Collins.*

Progression through the life cycle will be driven by:

- Changing technology or new products (eg telexes being replaced by faxes)
- Saturation of demand (eg once most households have acquired a microwave oven, demand will reduce to replacement levels).
- Changing consumer preferences (eg reduced consumption of red meat through changing attitudes to diet).

There will also be occasions where the product is 'born again', usually driven by a reversal in consumer preferences. Bicycles are a good example, with the product being well into decline in the 1970s. The rediscovery of the bicycle, more as a form of exercise than of transport, led to a revival of growth.

Example

American drive-in cinemas first appeared in Australian capital cities in the early 1950s. As is typical with new ideas, it took time to introduce this new American craze to Australians. Promotion was concentrated at attracting those people willing to innovate (the young, and those already introduced to the idea through American films). The product was fairly basic – a bulldozed paddock, screen and shed, with little else. The early prices were relatively high, creating some profits and attracting new operators.

By the mid 1950s, drive-in cinemas had moved into the growth phase. New drive-ins sprung up in the cities and in every big country town across Australia. The customers became more diverse – 'come as you please in the family car'. As competition increased, the cinemas vied for customers by enhancing the service through barbecues, car-hops, and quality of films.

Drive-ins moved into the mature part of the cycle in the early 1960s. The market for drive-ins reached saturation point. Those people who were likely to visit a drive-in had done so. Competition concentrated on stealing each others customers, creating return visits and earning more out of each customer by providing new and varied services.

Decline occurred in the seventies and eighties with the improvement of TV programs and the rising standard and comfit of cinemas. Drive-ins sort to capture the continued interest of users through: theme sessions, free extras, multiple sessions for the price of one etc, however these generated erratic patronage rather than the regular use of the sixties. Profitability declined.

More recently the introduction of videos and now DVDs combined with the high opportunity cost of land has resulted in the demise of the drive-in by 2000.

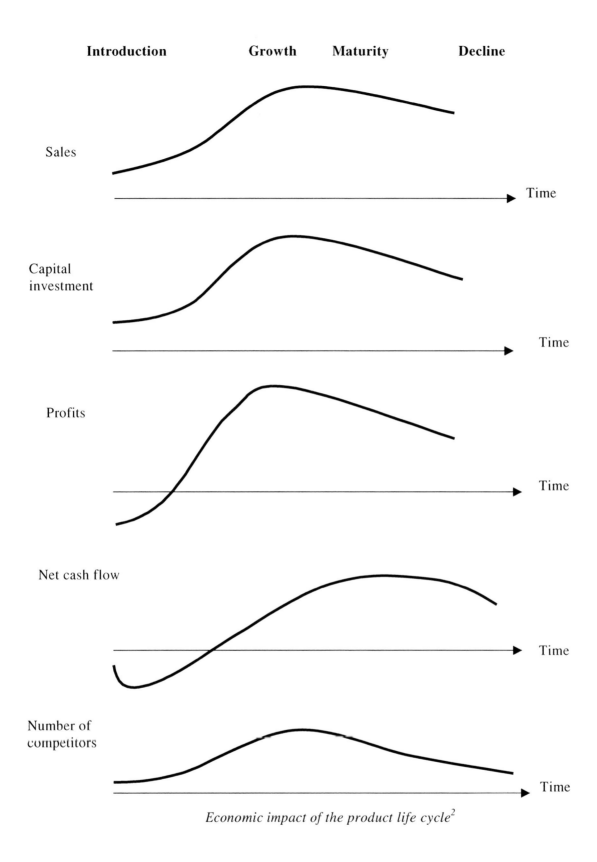

Economic impact of the product life cycle[2]

---

[2] Lewis, Morkel, Hubbard, 'Australian Strategic Management', Prentice Hall, 1993

Product Life Cycle Characteristics & Responses

1. Contestable Markets

If entry into an industry is easy and low cost to enter and easy and cheap for entrant to leave then the industry is considered highly contestable and firms will continue to enter into the industry as long as they perceive there is profit to be earned. If the entry is costly or difficult (ie due to scale of production, ability to access raw resources) or if exit from the industry is costly or difficult (i.e. redundancy payments, low resale or scrap value of equipment) or if there are some economy of scales then the firm will be less willing to enter the market unless they perceive the profits are large enough to make the risk warranted. If in a perfectly contestable industry it can transpire that there is just one firm if it is a natural monopoly ie more than one would make both unprofitable.

A perfectly contestable market is one, which is vulnerable to hit and run entry and exit because entry is easy and costless and because it is easy and cheap for the entrant to pick up their marbles and depart if the market should prove to be less attractive than was anticipated.

Usually in a contestable market the product is homogeneous (same product for for all competitors) with a large number of firms all competing the supply the consumer. There are no long-run monopoly profits as new firms will continually enter the market if they perceive a chance of profits.

However sometimes, in a perfectly contestable industry if it transpires that just one firm can produce industry output most economically (natural monopoly) then in the long run the industry will prove to be a **monopoly**. If two or three firms prove to be economical then an **oligopoly** will exist.

A non perfectly contestable market is one in which there are:

- entry costs (eg capital requirements)
- exit costs (eg specialist expensive equipment)
- economies of scale

If the market is not contestable then there is increased likelihood that monopoly (bigger that normal) profits will accrue to the firms in the industry. The cost of entering or exiting the industry may act as a deterrent for new firms in enter the market so that firms already in the industry can charge prices higher (over a long period) than would exist under contestable conditions with out risk of new competition entering the industry.

Impact of the Five Industry Forces on the Australian Beer Industry[3]

The Australian Beer industry has been in slow decline since 1975 – Australians are drinking less beer. Notwithstanding this decline the beer industry has remained very profitable. Some insight into the continuing high levels of profitability can be gained through the Five Industry Forces Model.

Entry Barriers

The entry barriers for the beer industry are enormous. They include:

- Long-established and strong brands, the result of millions of dollars of past and present advertising expenditure (the two major brewers now spend about $60 million per annum in supporting and developing brand names)

- Difficulty in gaining access to the distribution system (pubs and bottle shops)

- High start up costs, both in setting up plant and in establishing brand and distribution.

- The likelihood of retaliation if a new entrant started to gain market share.

- Economies of scale in production, marketing and distribution, which would significantly disadvantage a new entrant in the early years of operations.

The strength of barriers was tested in 1986 when the UK brewer, Courage, decided to enter the Australian beer market. It unwisely selected Melbourne as its entry market in which Carlton & United Brewing (CUB) enjoyed an almost 100 per cent market share. CUB did not react kindly to the intentions of Courage, intensifying its advertising efforts and discouraging its publicans from stocking Courage. As the publicans were almost entirely dependent on CUB for their livelihoods, they took the prudent option and provided little encouragement to the new entrant. (This was an early and obvious case of unfair use of market power and inspired some of the later Trade Practices legislation – at the time the response was not illegal.)

After one year and heavy losses Courage had captured only 4% of the Victorian market, which was not sufficient to sustain the operation. Courage found it was virtually impossible to extend its distribution channels other than by actually acquiring or building its own pubs – an expensive way of gaining market share. After four years of significant losses and little progress, Courage realised the futility of its efforts and returned to Britain poorer and wiser. Ironically, eighteen years later, Courage was acquired by Elders/CUB in their attempt to enter the UK beer market. This attempt was not much more successful and in 1995 Courage was sold, at a loss for Elders/CUB of approximately $1 billion.

---

[3] Bruce, R. (2000) Creating Your Strategic Future, Harper Business, Sydney pp61–67.

Rivalry among existing competitors

Over the last few decades the beer industry has been dominated by the two large national brewing groups (CUB/Elders/Foster's and Castlemaine/Bond/Lion Nathan), with minor competition from three smaller regional brewers (South Australian Brewing (SAB) in South Australia, Cascade in Tasmania and Power Brewing in Queensland from 1988) Cascade and power have since been acquired by Foster's (1993) and SAB's interest in South Australia by Lion Nathan (1994). Other boutique brewers (Hahn and Matilda Bay) have also been acquired by the majors.

With only two major competitors in an industry with declining sales, significant price competition would serve little purpose. The principal area of competition has been advertising. The need to avoid price competition and to maximize profits was further reinforced by the over extended financial position of the two competitors (Bond and Elders) during the second half of the 1980s. Maximised profits from Australian beer sales were crucial to survival – gaining market share through price cutting was not an acceptable strategy for either company.

The purchase of Castlemaine Tooheys by Lion Nathan in 1992 initiated a struggle by Lion Nathan to regain lost market share and this resulted in some price discounting. During 1994 the level of discounting appeared to abate and the two majors have now reverted to competing through new product launches (eg Ice brewed beer and advertising, rather than on price)

Substitutes

The most direct substitute for beer is wine, and much of the decline in beer consumption during the 1980s can be explained by consumers switching from beer to wine. The period of strongest decline for the beer industry was the period of strongest growth for wine. Historically, the reasons for switching were partly related to price, but more recently wine prices have increased faster than beer prices. While some substitution continues, it is occurring at a much slower rate and is driven by the increasing sophistication of consumer taste. In the past few years non-alcoholic substitutes have become more important, as many consumers are preferring to drink less alcohol.

The shift to other substitutes, including wine, continues to be an issue for the beer industry. As most of the switching is driven by preference, and not price, the impact is reflected more in lower sales than in lower prices.

Bargaining power of buyers

The important buyers of beer are the publicans and they have always been at the mercy of brewers. In Victoria, Western Australia and Tasmania there has been only one principal brewer; in the other states only two. As a consequence, publicans have little opportunity to shop around, and have consistently had the supply dictated to them (eg payment for beer supplies within 14 days). The very low bargaining power of the publicans is further exacerbated when pubs are owned by, or tied to, the brewer.

The bargaining power of suppliers

The bargaining power of suppliers (packaging, malt, hops etc.) is also limited. The major packaging companies, Amcor and Southcorp, may have some ability to negotiate, but in the final analysis the brewers have the upper hand. This was demonstrated by the decision of Foster's (previously CUB) to switch canning contracts away form Southcorp in 1993, leaving Southcorp with a large amount of unused canning capacity.

Not surprisingly, with the five industry forces operating in such a subdued way, the industry has remained one of Australia's most profitable.

Power Brewing Limited – exploiting damaged entry barriers

The high level of profitability achieved in the beer industry will always make it a tantalizing prospect for aspiring entrants. The almost impenetrable entry barriers permit the dominance of the majors to continue, with occasional but insignificant challenges from small boutique brewers (eg the Matilda Bay Brewing Company with Red Back beer). The importance of entry barriers and the way in which they operate are highlighted by Power Brewing's entry into the Queensland beer market in 1988.

After Bond Corporation acquired Castlemaine Perkins in 1985, the company made a series of fundamental strategic and marketing blunders which seriously eroded its dominant position in the industry. These included:

- Changing the name of the company from Castlemaine Perkins to Bond Brewing.

- Changing the address on the cans to a Perth address.

- Removing the famous Castlemaine Perkins sign which was a Brisbane city landmark

- Reducing sponsorship to local sporting activities.

Queenslanders are notoriously loyal to Queensland and the XXXX brand was an important Queensland icon enjoying 81% of the Queensland beer market. Bond's misplaced belief in national beer brands was dramatically destroying what was probably the strongest brand in Australia and, in doing so, it was lowering the entry barriers.

Bernie Power, a Queensland publican, was aware of the alienation being experienced by the Queensland public. He was also aware of the dislike most Queensland publicans had for Bond Brewing, which had exploited its bargaining power over publicans to an excessive level for many years. In 1988, Power formed Power Brewing Ltd with shares offered to the Queensland public. When Powers Bitter was launched late 1988 it captured 10 per cent of the Queensland market in one month, with the company having to ration supplies. It was enthusiastically supported by the publicans, who were relieved to have an alternative supplier. Power expanded production and captured 20 per cent of the market within 18 months of its launch. In contrast to Courage in Melbourne, Power had succeeded in penetrating the enormous barriers of brand and consumer acceptance, as well as gaining the support of the publicans. None of this would have been possible without the mismanagement and insensitivity of Bond Brewing in actively dismantling the entry barriers.

While it is sometimes tempting to maximise profitability by reducing the ongoing investment in a brand or by aggressively exploiting bargaining power over the distribution channels, this approach will often weaken the entry barriers and seriously imperil the long-term position of the business.

Look after the entry barriers and, in turn, they will look after you.

Sequel: Bond Corporation ultimately failed and the XXXX brand was taken over by Lion Nathan Ltd, which managed the brand back to is former dominant position. Power was astute enough to recognize the challenge of competing with a well-managed company with a dominant brand and large-scale economies. He sold the Queensland brewing operations to Foster's at a handsome profit.

Summarising the impact of the five forces in the Australian beer industry

> - **Threat of new Entrants**
> - Very high entry barriers
> - Strong, long established brands with high ongoing advertising expenditure
> - Established distribution systems
> - High start-up costs
> - Economies of scale particularly in marketing and distribution
> - Likelihood of retaliation
>
> *Intensity of force and its impact on profitability*
>
> $^2/_{10}$

> **5. Bargaining Power of suppliers**
> - The brewing companies are very powerful buyers of all supplies and can dictate terms
> - They have the power to switch suppliers, even with large packaging companies
>
> *Intensity of force and its impact on profitability*
>
> $^2/_{10}$

> **2. Rivalry among existing competitors**
> - With only two major in a declining market, there are strong arguments to avoid price competition
> - Competition has mostly been through advertising and new product launches
> - Prices have in the long term increased faster than inflation
>
> *Intensity of force and its impact on profitability*
>
> $^4/_{10}$

> **4. Bargaining power of buyers**
> - The two major brewers can dictate terms to the publicans
> - The publicans (of whom there are thousands) have little opportunity to switch suppliers and, more or less have to accept what is offered.
>
> *Intensity of force and its impact on profitability*
>
> $^1/_{10}$

> **3. Threat of substitute products or services**
> - In the past, wine has been the important substitute
> - More recently non-alcoholic beverages are becoming important
> - Substitutes affect volume more than price
>
> *Intensity of force and its impact on profitability*
>
> $^6/_{10}$

> **4a. Influence of end consumer**
> - The strength of beer brands limits the power of publicans

Strategic Practice Exercise

What are the forces driving industry competition in the airline industry? Read the following paragraphs. Using Porter's approach to industry analysis, evaluate each of the six forces to ascertain what drives the level of competitive intensity in this industry.

In recent years, the airline industry has become increasingly competitive. Since being deregulated during the 1990's in the Australia, long established airlines such as Ansett, have gone out of business as new upstarts like Virgin Blue have successfully entered the market. It appeared that the emphasis had changed from a focus on passenger travel to a transport haulage focus. Added to this was the fear created by the September 11 World trade center catastrophe and terrorism which had may the public much more weary of air travel and the Bali Bombing the following year. Which saw a drop in overseas travel and tourist coming to Australia. People are less willing to travel.

The government had recently announces a new cost to be imposed on the airline terminals and air lines for improvements to security required to scan all luggage going through the airport. Australia's postal service 'Post' has also been requested to have customers who require packages to go overseas to provide identification otherwise the postal article will require scanning and thus be delayed.

These increased security measures are on top of the already extensive number of taxes imposed on the traveling public with the air port taxes, the Ansett Tax, GST etc A fight from Adelaide to Melbourne may cost as low as $125 of which a third is the taxes or levies.

International carriers have permission to pick up passengers at capital city airports and so compete against the two Australian domestic lines. Virgin Blue has been able to enter the market at lower costs by offering Internet bookings with additional charges for any part of their service above the basic seat. With additional charges for meals, telephone bookings etc that where once considered 'part of the service.' Virgin Blue changes the market expectations.

Qantas to compete looked at reduced their costs by instituting a cap on travel agent commissions. Travel agencies were livid at this cut in their livelihood, but they needed the airlines' business in order to offer customers a total travel package. Servicing of planes was moved overseas where labour costs where lower. Loyalty programs and club membership is used by Qantas to retain and encourage high return passengers, such as business class and corporate customers, to use their service.

Globally it seemed as though every nation had to have its own airline for national prestige. These state-owned airlines were expensive, but the governments subsidised them with money and supporting regulation. For example, a foreign airline was normally only allowed to fly into one of a country's airports – forcing travellers to switch to the national airline to go to other cities. During the 1970s and 1980s, however, many countries began privatising their airlines as governments tried to improve their budgets. To be viable in an increasingly global industry, national or regional airlines were forced to form alliances and even purchase and airline in another country or region. For example, in December 1992 Qantas formed a strategic alliance with British Airways (BA) in order to obtain not only Australian/Europe destinations, but also Asian travel routes, thus making it one of the few global alliances. British Airways which already has a 22 percent stake in the Qantas has expressed an interest in raising its holding. Australia's foreign investment rules control the portion of the carrier that can be owned by foreign companies to 49 percent and 25 percent for any single overseas airline. Qantas has been pressing for a relaxation of the rules, which it sees as a barrier to growth however in August 2002 the government rejected any changes to its rules.

In October 2002 Qantas took a 22.5 per cent cornerstone shareholding in Air New Zealand.

Costs were still relatively high for all of the world's major airlines because of the high cost of new airplanes. Just one new jet plane cost anywhere from $25 million to $100 million. By the 1990s, only three airframe manufacturers provided almost all of the commercial airliners: Boeing, Airbus, and McDonnell Douglas. Major airlines were forced to purchase new planes because they were more fuel efficient, safer, and easier to maintain. Airlines that chose to stay with an older fleet of planes had to deal with higher fuel and maintenance costs-factors that often made it cheaper to buy new planes. This was demonstrated by the demise of Ansett, due in part to its high cost of maintaining a fleet of old planes from a variety of manufacturers. In 2002 Qantas' launches new international subsidiary airline under the historical name of 'Australian Airlines'.

1. Evaluate each of the forces driving competition in the airline industry:

Threat of New Entrants	High	Medium	Low	_____
Rivalry Among Existing Firms	High	Medium	Low	_____
Threat of Substitutes	High	Medium	Low	_____
Bargaining Power of Buyers/ Distributors	High	Medium	Low	_____
Bargaining Power of Suppliers	High	Medium	Low	_____
Relative Power of Other Stakeholders	High	Medium	Low	_____

2. Which of these forces is changing? What will this mean to the overall level of competitive intensity in the airline industry in the future? Would you invest or look for a job in this industry?

Activity

ENVIRONMENTAL ANALYSIS

Consider these issues under the following headings

- Political
- Economic
- Sociol-cultural
- Technical
- Legal/political
- Pluralistic

How might issues in these areas affect the organisations or its industry? In summary are external influences supporting or retarding the future growth of the industry?

INDUSTRY ANALYSIS

Analyse each of the five forces in Porter's model

- threat of new entrants
- supplier power
- buyer power
- substitutes
- industry rivalry

Draw a conclusion about how profitable the industry is.

- Why do you believe it is profitable/unprofitable?
- What trends exist?
- Who are the key competitors in this industry?
- What is the basis on which they compete?
- How successful are they?
- What are the critical success factors for an organisation to operate in this industry?

Michael Porter's three generic strategies

Porter recommends **three generic strategies** to out-perform competitors or maintain a market position against competition.

1.   Overall Cost Leadership

- produce the same/better quality at less cost than anyone else. Enjoy greater profits or - in a price war - stay in the market, profitably, with reduced prices.

This may be because they can produce higher volumes, which gives them economies of scale, or it might be because their overheads are lower (working from home, virtual organisation).

Activity

Why is Virgin Blue able to get its overhead costs such as terminal hire, administration lower than its major competitor Qantas ?

How does Shopfast (see http://www.shopfast.com.au/) compete against Coles and Woolworth?

This may revolutionise a firm where industry competition has been sluggish. Competitors may be ill-prepared - mentally, economically, operationally - to minimise costs, eg steel, retail banking, lager, an in-patient day.

2.   Differentiation

- implies a range of better/different product/service (or perceived as different) from others.

Quality imperatives demand a strategy equating the product with "desirable" quality standards. Differentiation can earn above average profits even in slow growth or declining market.

3.   Market Niche/Segmentation -

- focusing on

1.   a section or group of the buying public, or

2.   a segment of a product line, or

3.   an area of a geographic market

Premise - we can service a narrow target more effectively than rivals who compete more broadly. Low cost and differentiation will still be required for the niche.

Activity

Compare Mercedes Benz, Hyundai and Holden Utes. Which fits which strategy?

Stuck in the Middle

The Porter recommendation is to **avoid getting caught in the middle.**

If you pursue one of these strategies you cannot effectively pursue the others. For example if you are a supermarket who is looking to be a cost leader (lowest cost) then you can not do things that add costs to your organisation such as providing a free home delivery service, refurbish the supermarket periodically etc. In stead you are looking at getting those costs as low as possible by employing more under 18 cashers, joining a bulk buying group to get discounts.

Activity

Why did John Martins fail?

UNIT 8

RESOURCE-BASED MODEL

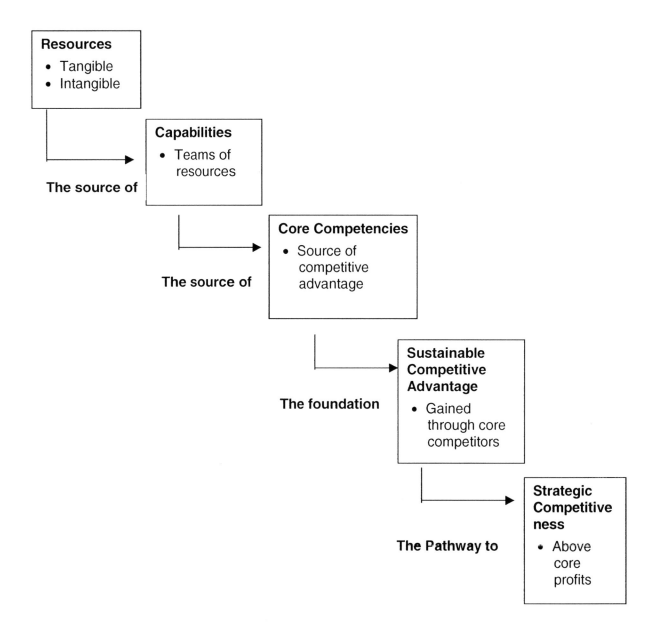

Core Competencies

Your organisation and the unit or functional area you manage has certain resources: Human, Financial, Physical and Intangible assets.

System thinking shows that it is how these resources interact and relate to each other that gives them value. The resource based model is concerned with how we recognize those assets and your organisation can bundle the assets so that they allow the organisation or unit to compete more effectively.

Porter's view of understanding the industry and what position your unit holds in that industry is important but as a division or unit you need to understand also your resources and how you can use them to best position your organisation.

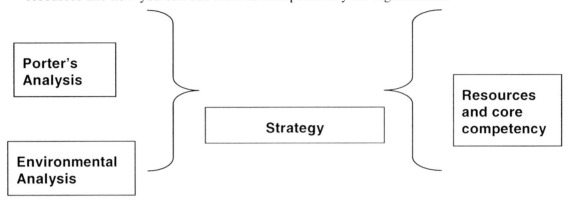

Resources

Below is a list of resources, not all resources in an organisation are of equal value. It is necessary to pick those resources that are important, those that allow you to operate effectively.

For a resource to qualify as the basis for an effective strategy, it must pass a number of external market tests of its value:

1.   The test of inimitability: Is the resource hard to copy?

2.   The test of durability: How quickly does this resource depreciate?

3.   The test of appropriability: Who captures the value that the resources create?

4.   The test of substitutability: Can a unique resource be trumped by a different resource?

5.   The test of competitive superiority: Whose resource is really better?

Source: Collis, David J & Montgomery, Cynthia A, Competing on Resources Strategy in the 1990s, HBR July-Aug, 1995, p118-128.

Tangible Resources[1]	
Financial Resources	• The firm's borrowing capacity • The firm's ability to generate internal funds
Physical Resources	• Sophistication and location of a firm's plant and equipment • Access to raw materials
Human Resources	• The training, experience, judgment, intelligence, insights, adaptability, commitment, and loyalty of a firm's individual managers and workers.
Organisational Resource	• The firm's formal reporting structure and its formal planning, controlling, and coordinating systems

Intangible Resources[2]	
Technological Resource	• Stock of technology such as patents, trademarks, copyrights and trade secrets • Knowledge required to apply it successfully
Resources for Innovation	• Technical employees • Research facilities

Reputation	• Reputation with customers
	  ▪ Brand name
	  ▪ Perceptions of product quality, durability, and reliability
	• Reputation with suppliers
	  ▪ For efficient, effective, supportive, and mutually beneficial interactions and relationships

---

[1] Adapted from Hitt, Michael, A., Ireland, R., Duane, Hoskisson, Robert, E. (1999) Strategic Management competitiveness and Globalization, 3rd ed.

2 Adapted from Hitt, Michael, A., Ireland, R., Duane, Hoskisson, Robert, E. (1999) Strategic Management competitiveness and Globalization, 3rd ed.

Four Criteria for Determining Strategic Capabilities[3]	
Value Capabilities	• Help a firm neutralise threats or exploit opportunities
Rare Capabilities	• Are not possessed by many others
Costly to Imitate Capabilities	• Historical: A unique and a valuable organisational culture or brand name
	• Ambiguous cause: The causes and uses of a competence are unclear
	• Social complexity: Interpersonal relationships, trust and friendship among managers, suppliers, and customers
Non-substitutable Capabilities	• No strategic equivalent

Capability

Resources are usually bundled together to enable the business to provide some output, service or product. This is summarised in a statement of what the unit is capable of or **capability**.

For example

> *High level of customer service for Qantas Booking area will be the resulting capability of bundling the skills of staff, an effective computerised booking system, a well designed office system.*

Resources are the source of a firm's capabilities. Capabilities are the source of a firm's core competencies, which are the foundation for the development of sustainable competitive advantage.

To be a source of competitive advantage, a capability must allow a firm to:

1. Perform a particular primary or support activity in a manner that is superior to the manner in which competing companies perform it or,

2. Perform a value-creating activity that no competitor can perform.

---

[3] Adapted from Hitt, Michael, A., Ireland, R., Duane, Hoskisson, Robert, E. (1999) Strategic Management competitiveness and Globalization, 3rd ed.

The capability must therefore be:

- Valuable
- Rare
- Costly to imitate
- Non-substitutionable.

Core Competencies

- They should provide the organisation with the potential to access a wide variety of markets with a wide variety of products and services.

- A core competency should create value as defined by the customer.

- Core competencies are sustainable.

- A core competency is difficult for a competitor to copy.

Competencies vs. Core Competencies vs. Distinctive Competencies[4]

- A **competence** is an *internal activity* that a company performs *better* than other internal activities.

- A **core competence** is a well-performed internal activity that is *central*, not peripheral, to a company's *strategy, competitiveness, and profitability.*

- A **distinctive competence** is a *competitively valuable activity* that a company **performs better than its rivals.**

---

[4] © The McGraw-Hill Companies Inc.,1998.

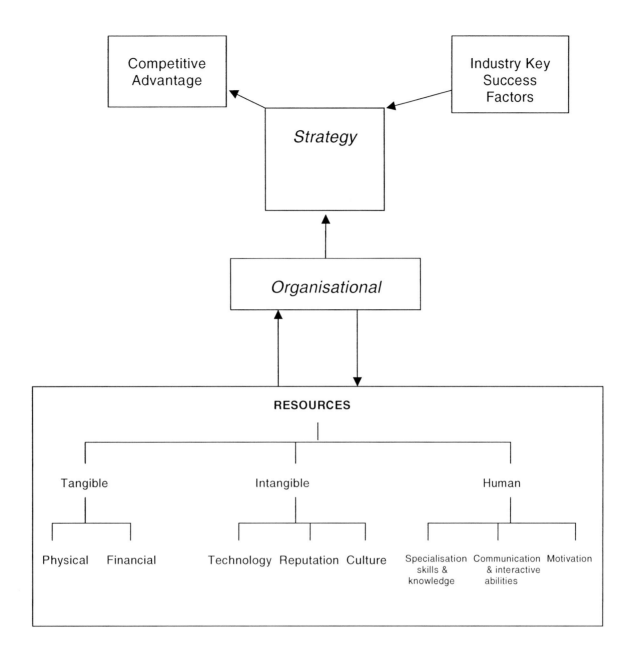

How far can the unit's valuable resources be extended across markets?

Three common strategic errors:

- Managers tend to over estimate the transferability of specific assets and capabilities

- Managers overestimate their ability to compete in highly profitable industries

- Managers assume that leverage in generic resources will be a major source of competitive advantage in a new market – regardless of the specific competitive dynamics of that market.

Uses of the Resource Model

- Effective use of resources: sell those assets that do not enhance your core competency or core capabilities, build/enhance those that do.

- Match your core capabilities and core competence with what your corporate strategy and industry analysis is telling you.

CORE CAPABILITIES
➢ Safety is a strong capability as an impeccable record speaks for itself. Financial management is critical to any business but if it came at the cost of safety, Qantas would lose a major advantage over its competitors. Safety is difficult to replicate once a recordable loss has been experienced by a competitor. It is also easily lost and must be carefully marketed so as not to attach to the brand too heavily.
➢ As a truly integrated international and domestic carrier, Qantas offers a continuation of service from domestic to the broadest range of overseas destinations of the two current Australian airlines. Messages such as continued safety are carried through to international travellers through this extended brand exposure.
➢ Qantas has an excellent presence in the Asia Pacific region, the fastest growing international tourist destination in the world. This coupled with Qantas' excellent branding position places them in a strong position for inbound and outbound passenger growth. The issue of reach into markets within Asia, internal flights, must be addressed if it is to become a major regional player. Currently, reach is a weakness yet presence, brand, is a strength.

> ➤ Strategic alliances with major global airlines such as British Airways and American extended the reach of the company and also offer a continued service with a "Qantas approved" airline. This is likely to be the most critical step for Qantas as they compete into the year 2000 and beyond.

> ➤ Fleet maintenance and the average fleet age proves effective asset management. The safety perception is most likely built on the basis of fleet age and condition and will become, it is isn't already, a major competitive advantage in the future.

CORE COMPETENCIES:-

The special knowledge, skills, and technological know-how that distinguish you from other firms...

plus

STRATEGIC PROCESSES:-

The business processes you use to deliver your special know-how in the form of products, services, and other results that have high value to customers and other stakeholders

equals

CORE CAPABILITIES

The most critical and most distinctive resources a company possesses, and the most difficult to copy when effectively linked with appropriate strategic targets in a value chain and ends with the company's key stakeholders.

For Qantas to have the necessary strategic core capabilities they should meet the definition laid down by Hubbard, Pocknee & Taylor 'Practical Australian Strategy Prentice Hall (1996):

- It must be of value to the customer
- It must be better than that of most competitors
- It must be difficult to replicate.

UN*IT* 9

SWOT ANALY*SIS*

SWOT stands for **S**trength, **W**eaknesses, **O**pportunity and **T**hreats. This is a tool to help summarise the organisation's internal and external environment. It allows you to draw some conclusions about how best to deploy your resources in light of the units internal and external situation.

You develop strategies from the process of:

- Building on the strengths
- Minimising the weaknesses
- Avoiding the threats
- Utilising the opportunities

Strength and weaknesses are about the internal resources and capabilities of the unit/organisation. The threats and opportunities are about the external environment.

The SWOT is a simple tool to use but a hard tool to use effectively. Make sure that the statements you make are meaningful and summaries important issues.

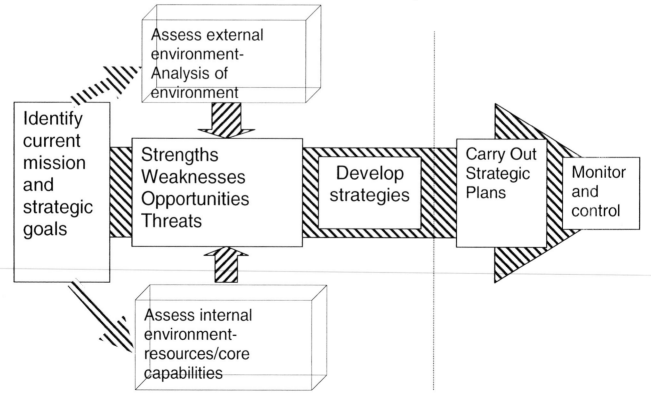

Evaluating an organisation's/unit's strengths and weaknesses

Organisational Strengths Skills or capabilities that enable an organisation to conceive of and implement its strategies.

Organisation Weaknesses Skills or capabilities that prevent an organisation from achieving and implement its strategies.

These are about the **internal resources and capabilities** of the unit/organisation. The strengths and weaknesses can be divided into **common** (a capability possessed by a large number of competing organisations) and **distinctive competencies** (core competencies).

Identifying resource strengths and distinctive capabilities

Your **competitive position** is based on how well your mix of internal resources and capabilities have given you a core competency.

A strength is something a firm does well or a characteristics that enhances its competitiveness

- Valuable competencies or know-how
- Valuable physical assets
- Valuable human assets
- Valuable organisational assets
- Valuable intangible assets
- Important competitive capabilities
- An attribute that places the unit in a stronger competitive position
- Strategic alliances

These are those aspects of the organisation that the organisation does well. The can be divided into those that affect the organisation's efficiency (operational effectiveness) and those things that affect its effectiveness (competitive position)

Achieving or extending best practice in activities by:

- Employing the most up-to-date equipment and information technology
- Eliminating waste, defects and delays
- Stimulating continuous organisational improvement
- Operating closer to the productivity frontier

These allow you to stay in the game; they do not give you a distinctive advantage over other competitors.

Examples Of Operational Effectiveness measure

If your organisation adopts these measures to improve its efficiency and your competitors don't, then you will earn more profits and eat aware at competitors share of the market just because you do things better. Alternatively if your competitors are adopting these methods then they will be able to attract your customers and clients by being more efficiently and better than you. So to remain in the industry you need to adopt **best practice**. So the following methods tend to go across industries:

- Total quality Management (TQM)
- Benchmarking
- Re-engineering
- Virtual corporation
- Learning organisation
- Network Organisation
- Strategic Business Units
- Self directed teams
- Flexible Manufacturing Systems
- Just in time

Evaluating an organisation's/unit's opportunities and threats

Opportunities Areas in the environment that if exploited, may generate high performance

Threats Areas in the environment that increase the difficulty of an organisation/units achieving maximum performance.

This requires you analyse the external environment and to utilise Porter's five elements. The opportunities and threats are the conclusion you have developed.

Operational effectiveness vs. Strategic positioning

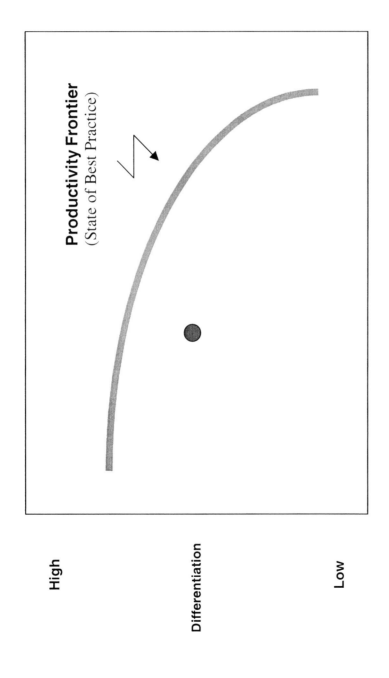

Productivity Frontier
(State of Best Practice)

High

Differentiation

Low

Relative Cost Position

Source: M Porter, 1999.

Creating Strategies

SWOT is a useful tool to help formulate strategies.

SWOT analysis –What to look for[1]			
Potential Resource Strengths	**Potential Resource Weaknesses**	**Potential Company Opportunities**	**Potential External Threats**
• Powerful strategy • Strong financial condition • Strong Brand Name / Image / Reputation • Widely recognised market leader • Proprietary technology • Cost advantages • Strong advertising • Product innovation skills • Good customer service • Better product quality • Alliances or joint ventures	• No clear strategic direction • Obsolete facilities • Weak balance sheet excessive debt • Higher overall costs than rivals • Missing some key skills / competencies • Subpar profits • Internal operating problems • Falling behind in R&D • Too narrow product line • Weal marketing skills	• Serving additional customer groups • Expanding to new geographic areas • Expanding product line • Transferring skills to new products • Vertical integration • Openings to take market share from rivals • Acquisition of rivals • Alliances or joint ventures to expand coverage • Openings to exploit new technologies • Openings to extend brand name / image	• Entry of potent new competitors • Loss of sales to substitutes • Slowing market growth • Adverse shifts in exchange rates and trade policies • Costly new regulations • Vulnerability to the business cycle • Growing leverage of customers or suppliers • Shift in buyer needs for product • Demographic changes

---

1 © McGraw-Hill Companies Inc 1998.

Checklist - Analysis of strengths and weaknesses

MARKET POSITION

- markets in which your company is operating
- market share (in relation to major competitors)
- trends in market share
- quality and characteristics of your products
- consumers'/customers' awareness of and preference for your company and its products
- degree of co-operation and support by distributors
- competitiveness of your pricing strategy
- expertise and experience of your marketing staff
- opportunities for product innovation
- economies of scale and your experience in the marketing area
- effectiveness of your sales force
- reliability and cost effectiveness of your physical distribution system
- patents or licences owned by the company

MARKETING

- resources allocated to accomplish the marketing task
- allocation of resources to markets, sales territories, distribution channels, product lines, etc
- profitability of markets, sales territories, distribution channels, product lines
- your marketing planning process
- your marketing control procedures
- your marketing information system
- marketing training, incentives, etc
- your pricing procedures
- use of price promotions
- use of distribution channels
- sales force size and expertise
- impact of advertising and promotion
- use of sales promotion
- use of Public Relations

PURCHASING

- expertise of your purchasing department/or officer
- (guaranteed) access to raw materials
- sourcing of raw material (multiple sourcing, contracts, etc)
- your standing with suppliers
- economies of scale in purchasing

PRODUCTION

- flexibility of production equipment
- modular manufacturing method
- level of technology used
- economies of scale and your experience in the production area
- capacity utilisation
- quality and reliability of equipment used
- breakdowns, delays, etc (accident or due to necessary maintenance work)

Checklist - Analysis of Opportunities and Threats

PART I: THE MACRO-ENVIRONMENT

POLITICAL AND LEGAL

Political and legal factors which have direct impact on your industry, or an indirect impact through suppliers or distributors.

Government Interventions
- price regulations
- import restrictions
- design rules
- pollution standards
- hygiene regulations (eg. in food or pharmaceutical industries)
- consumer protection legislation
- industry subsidies or protection
- legal requirements affecting consumption (eg. seatbelt legislation)
- anti-trust regulations
- export market development grants
- NIES programs and services

Rates, Taxes and Investment Incentives

- investment incentives, including research & development incentives and grants
- taxes, duties and government levies
- investment allowance, depreciation rules
- private income tax affecting consumers' disposable income

INDUSTRY ASSOCIATIONS

Union actions which have a direct impact on your industry, or an indirect impact by affecting suppliers or distributors.

- wage demands
- strike actions
- work hours
- additional commitments to employee welfare, health, safety
- additional retirement benefits
- co-operative worker arrangements - industrial democracy

PART II: THE INDUSTRY

DEMAND

- demand for products or services (market size and growth)
- key differences between market segments and growth of different market segments
- usage of products or services
- seasonality of demand
- market life-cycle (is it a new market, a growing market, a mature market or a declining market?)

SUPPLY

- total capacity and capacity utilisation in industry
- risks in supply of raw materials, ancillary services (eg. transport) or energy
- supply of labour and skill levels available
- capital supply

COMPETITIVE ANALYSIS

- number and size of (major) competitors
- financial strength of competitors
- skill levels and commitment of competitors' workforce
- leadership qualities of competitors' management
- dominance of competitor(s)
- concentration or fragmentation of industry

- key differences between competitors
- cost structure of major competitors
- location in relation to raw materials, labour, energy and markets
- competitors' extent of experience with the market, the products, etc.
- cost advantages such as patents, licenses, etc.
- exit barriers (making it hard to leave the industry)
- entry barriers (making it hard to enter the industry as a new competitor)
- economies of scale
- extent of differentiation between competitive products
- access to distribution channels
- pressure from substitute products
- bargaining power of buyers
- bargaining power of suppliers

PART III: CONCLUSION

- critical factors for the success of the industry in general and the success of a company operating in this industry in specific
- profitability and growth perspectives in the industry and of major competitors

David Jones/Grace Bros Swot Analysis

Potential Internal Strengths

- Acknowledged market leader in customer service
- Perception that it is different from its competitors

  "There's no other store like David Jones"

- Strong public image
- Skilled financial backing
- Customer loyalty
- Focused marketing strategy
- Wide product offerings

Potential Internal Weaknesses

- Some obsolete equipment (tills, stock recording)
- Deep resistance to change (identified by present staff)
- Poor track record in implementing change (noted by high turnover of senior management)
- Lacks general appeal in staff morale (weekend trading hours, overtime, lack of promotion opportunities)

Potential External Opportunities

- Increase appeal to wider community

- Take advantage of decentralisation and urban focus (shopping centre growth, etc.)

- Possible further deregulation of trading hours – more expensive for small traders, therefore possible competitive advantage for David Jones)

- Continuing expansion of product lines

- Favourable changes to award rates, conditions, etc.

Potential External Threats and Weaknesses

- Growth of direct competitors

- Keep of similar organisations into top end of market

- Threat of a slow economic growth

- Possibility of future industrial unrest

- Demographic shifts (money required to operate in other areas as urban sprawl continues)

- Changing buyer needs, and tastes

- The need for the organisation to appeal to investors (may affect managerial decision making)

Key Elements of Strategy

1. Strategy embodies management processes
2. Strategy involves managing the interface between an organisation and its external environment
3. Strategy involves managing organisational effectiveness
4. Strategy creates organisational flexibility
5. Effective strategy is innovative
6. Good strategies have the right time horizon
7. Strategy involves managing risk
8. Effective strategy is participative
9. Strategy involves managing organisational scope (trade offs)
10. Strategy occurs at different organisational levels
11. Strategy creates patterns of investment

Evaluating Strategic Options[2]

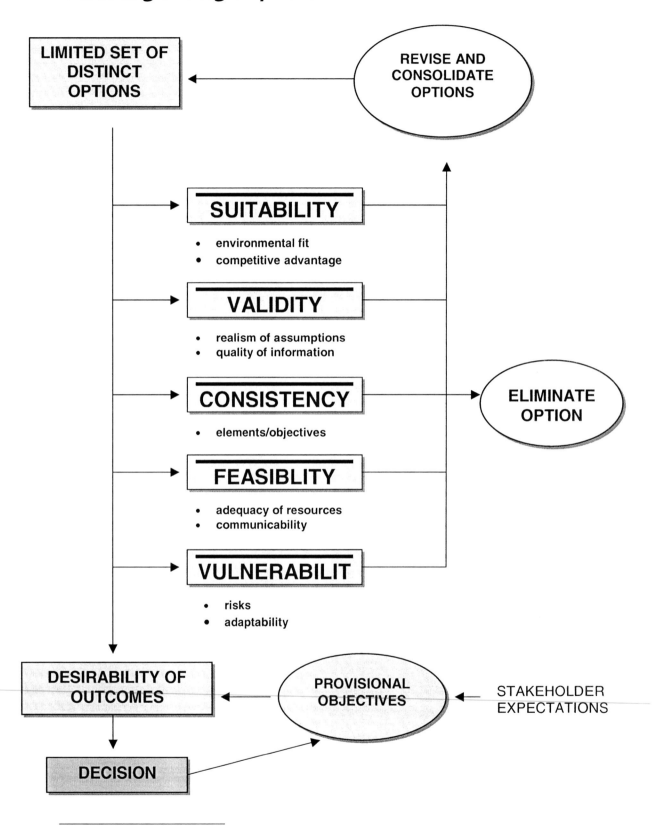

[2] G.S. Day, Analysis for Strategic Market Decision, 1986, p169.

Decision Criteria

☞

Suitability:	Is there a sustainable advantage?
Feasibility:	Do we have the skills, resources and commitment?
Vulnerability:	What are the risks and contingencies?
Financial Desirability:	How much economic value is created?

Refining Criteria

☞

Validity:	Are the assumptions valid?
Consistency:	Does the strategy hang together?
Communicability:	Is the strategy understandable

Strategies To Watch

- "Me too" or "copy-cat" strategies
- "Take-away" generic strategies
- Confrontational strategies
- Semi-commit strategies
- Drift strategies
- Hope-for-a-better-day strategies
- High downside strategies

Practical Issues In Strategy Evaluation

- Lack of industry analysis
- Overestimation of impact on market
- Underestimating the capabilities if competitors, especially small ones
- Limited consideration of the pros and cons of strategic options
- Little analysis of the cross effect between products and markets
- Lack of matching of required resources to support the strategy
- Insufficient and superficial Financial Analysis
- Problems of conflicts of opinion in the organisation
- Poor analysis of changes /impact on human resources etc.

Qantas Revisited

Strengths

Established brand name
Australian Product – 50% National Share
International connections – British Airways merger
Safety Record
Modern and efficient fleet
Compound growth 11.1%
Australian connection to Asia
Links with extensive route networks
Young fleet of jets in comparison to industry
Strict financial controls
Strong Management team

Weaknesses

British Airways alliance due to mature in 2003
Costs to maintain planes
Fixed costs need to be monitored-timing of ordering replacement planes (good times) delivery (bad times)
Government regulations within Australia and outside
Sensitivity to economic market fluctuations
Empty seats – innovation – could be dilled – increase revenue per seat
50% occupancy – increase
High operating leverage of industry
Earning sensitive to small shifts in revenue – driven by yield and seat factors
Reduced air fares mean lower yields

Opportunities

Declining cost of travel
Increased business travel into Aust
Leisure travel can be developed
Long distance travel packages to Asia and New Zealand
Asia Pacific region fastest growing international destination
Increase links with Asian economies
Bring people to Australia to visit family and friends on packages *23.8% outbound Vs 18% in)
Develop packages to bring business people into Australia (currently 9.6%)
50% occupancy can be increase by creative
Declining cost of air travel
Exploit travel out of Aust. During 2000 Olympics
Internet and web bookings
People working harder and longer, technology means to rest (i.e. mobile phone interruptions) therefore travel away from home for holidays
Link between passenger yield and traffic growth
Computerised yield management systems – pricing selling and availability – how to exploit

Threats

Economic turmoil strongly affects industry
Political conditions can reduce number of flights
Quadrupled growth in 24 years – can it be maintained
World recessions – share market is over buoyant – what it it crashes
War /Terrorism- Religious unrest
Yields declining at 2% per annum
Cost of replacements

UN*IT* 10

GLO*SS*ARY

Advertising	The use of communications media to gain favourable publicity for particular products and services.
Boundary spanning	Creating roles within the organisation that interface with important elements in the environment.
Buffering	Stockpiling either inputs into or outputs from a production or service process in order to cope with environmental fluctuations.
Capitalist economy	An economy in which economic activity is governed by market forces and the means of production are privately owned by individuals.
Ceremonial	A system of rites performed in conjunction with a single occasion or event.
Competitors	Other organisations that either offer or have a high potential of offering rival products or services.
Co-opting	Absorbing key members of important environmental elements into the leadership or policy-making structure of an organisation.
Corporate culture	A term sometimes used for organisation culture.
Customers and clients	Those individuals and organisations that purchase an organisations products and/or services.
Direct interlock	A situation in which two companies have a director in common.
Domain shifts	Changes in the mix of products and services offered so that an organisation will interface with more favourable environmental elements.
Economic element	The systems of producing, distributing and consuming wealth.
Environmental complexity	The number of elements in an organisation's environment and their degree of similarity.

Environmental dynamism	The rate and predictability of change in the elements of an organisation's environment.
Environmental munificence	The extent to which the environment can support sustained growth and stability.
Environmental uncertainty	A condition of the environment in which future conditions affecting an organisation cannot be accurately assessed and predicted.
External environment	The major forces outside the organisation that have the potential of significantly impacting on the likely success of products or services.
Forecasting	The systematic effort to estimate future conditions.
Government agencies	Agencies that provide services and monitor compliance with laws and regulations at local, state or regional, and national levels.
Indirect interlock	A situation in which two companies each have a director on the board of a third company.
Interlocking directorates	A situation in which organisations share board members in common either directly or indirectly.
Internal environment	The general conditions that exist within an organisation.
International element	The developments in countries outside an organisations home country that have the potential of impacting on the organisation.
Joint venture	An agreement involving two or more organisations that arrange to produce a product or service jointly.
Labour supply	Those individuals who are potentially employable by an organisation.
Legal-political element	The legal and governmental systems within which an organisation must function.
Mega-environment	The broad conditions and trends in the societies within which an organisation operates
Natural selection model	A term sometimes used for the population ecology model.
Negotiating contracts	Seeking favourable agreements on matters of importance to the organisation.

Organisational culture	A system of shared values, assumptions, beliefs, and norms that unite the members of an organisation.
Population ecology model	A model that focuses on populations or groups of organisations and argues that environmental factors cause organisations with appropriate characteristics to survive and others to fail.
Public relations	The use of communications media to gain favourable publicity for particular products and services.
Rationing	Providing limited access to a product or service that is in high demand.
Recruiting	Attracting job candidates who meet the needs of the organisation.
Resource dependence model	A model that highlights organisational dependence on the environment for resources and argues that organisations attempt to manipulate the environment to reduce that dependence.
Rite	A relatively elaborate, dramatic, planned set of activities intended to convey cultural values of participants and, usually, an audience.
Smoothing	Taking actions aimed at reducing the impact of fluctuations, given the market.
Socialist economy	An economy in which the means of production are owned by the state and economic activity is coordinated by plan.
Sociocultural element	The attitudes, values, norms, beliefs, behaviours, and associated demographic trends that are characteristic of a given geographic area.
Story	A narrative based on true events, which sometimes may be embellished to highlight the intended value.
Suppliers	Those organisations and individuals that supply the resources an organisation needs to conduct its operations.
Symbol	An object, act, event, or quality that serves as a vehicle for conveying meaning.
Task environment	The specific outside elements with which an organisation interacts in the course of conducting its business.

Technological element	The current state of knowledge regarding the production of products and services.
Trade associations	Organisations composed of individuals or firms with common business concerns.